FROM AMMA'S HEART

Conversations with

Sri Mata Amritanandamayi Devi

Translated & Written by
Swami Amritaswarupananda

*This book is offered at the Lotus Feet of
our most beloved Amma,
the source of all beauty and love*

From Amma's Heart:
Conversations With Sri Mata Amritanandamayi Devi
Translated and Written by Swami Amritaswarupananda

Published by
Mata Amritanandamayi Mission Trust
Amritapuri P.O., Kollam, Kerala, INDIA 690 525
Email: inform@amritapuri.org, Website: www.amritapuri.org

Fifth Printing - October 2013

Type setting and layout
Amrita DTP, Amritapuri

Aum Amriteswaryai Namah

Foreword

Without verbal communication, human existence would be miserable. Exchanging ideas and sharing emotions are part and parcel of life itself. However, it is the silence that we acquire through prayer and meditation that really helps us find peace and true happiness in this noisy world of conflicting differences and competition.

In normal every day life, where people have to interact and communicate in numerous situations, observing silence is difficult. And even if our surroundings are conducive to quietude, remaining silent is not so easy. It can even drive ordinary human beings crazy. However, blissful silence is the true nature of divine personalities such as Amma.

Watching Amma deal with various situations and people all over the world, I have seen the grace and perfection with which She switches from one mood to another. One moment, Amma is the supreme Spiritual Master and, the next, the compassionate mother. Sometimes She takes the mood of a child, at others of an administrator. After advising CEOs, award-winning scientists and world leaders, She simply gets up and walks to the darshan hall, where She receives and consoles thousands of Her children from all walks of life. Generally, Amma spends Her whole day—and most of Her night—comforting Her children, listening to them, wiping their tears, infusing them with faith, confidence and strength. Throughout all this, Amma ever remains in Her natural serene state. She never gets tired. She never complains. Her face is always aglow with that radiant smile. Amma the extraordinary in ordinary form dedicates every moment of Her life to others.

What makes Amma different from us? What is the secret? From where does Her infinite energy and power come? Amma's presence reveals the answer to these questions so clearly and tangibly. Her words reaffirm it: "The beauty of your words, the charm in your actions, the allure of your movements all depend on the amount of silence you create within. Humans have the capacity to go deeper and deeper into that silence. The deeper you go, the closer you come to the Infinite."

That profound silence is the very core of Amma's existence. The unconditional love, unbelievable patience, extraordinary grace and purity—everything Amma embodies are extensions of the vast silence in which She revels.

There was a time when Amma wouldn't speak like She does today. Once, when asked about this, Amma said, "Even if Amma spoke, you wouldn't understand anything." Why? Because, as ignorant as we are, we cannot begin to comprehend the highest and subtlest experience in which Amma is established. Then why is Amma speaking? It is best to put it in Amma's own words: "If nobody guides the seekers of Truth, they may quit the path, thinking there is no such state as Self-realization."

In fact, Great Souls such as Amma would rather remain silent than talk about the reality behind this objective world of happenings. Amma very well knows that Truth, when conveyed through words, inevitably is distorted, and that our limited, ignorant minds will incorrectly interpret it in the way that least disturbs our ego. Even so, this embodiment of compassion speaks to us, answers our questions and clears our doubts, knowing full well our minds will only create more and more confusing questions. It is Amma's patience and untainted love for humanity that causes Her to keep responding to our silly queries. She will not stop until our minds, too, become blissfully silent.

In the conversations recorded in this book, Amma, the Master of Masters, is bringing Her mind down to the level of Her children, helping us obtain a glimpse of the changeless reality that serves as the substratum for the changing world.

I have been collecting these pearls of wisdom since 1999. Almost all the conversations and beautiful incidents herein were recorded during Amma's Western tours. Sitting by Amma's side during darshan, I have been trying to listen to the sweet, divine melodies of Amma's heart, which She is ever ready to share with Her children. Capturing the purity, simplicity and profundity of Amma's words is not easy. It is definitely beyond my capacity. However, by sheer merit of Her infinite compassion, I have been able to record these divine utterances and reproduce them here.

Like Amma Herself, Amma's words, too, have deeper dimension than immediately meets the eye—an infinite aspect that the ordinary human mind cannot grasp. I have to confess my own inability to fully understand and appreciate the deeper meaning of Amma's words. Our minds, which loiter in the trivial world of objects, cannot begin to comprehend that highest state of consciousness, from where Amma is speaking. That said, I strongly feel Amma's words contained herein are very special and somehow different from those found in previous books.

My earnest desire was to select and present Amma's beautiful and informal talks to Her children. It took me four years to collect them. Within is carried the whole universe. These words come from the depths of Amma's consciousness. So, just beneath their surface, is that blissful silence—Amma's true nature. Read with a deep feeling. Contemplate and meditate on that feeling and the words will reveal their inner meaning.

Dear readers, I am sure that the contents of this book will enrich and enhance your spiritual quest by clearing your doubts and purifying your minds.

Swami Amritaswarupananda
September 15th 2003

Purpose of Life

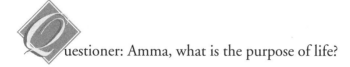

Questioner: Amma, what is the purpose of life?

Amma: It depends on your priorities and how you look at life.

Questioner: My question is what is the "real" purpose of life.

Amma: The real purpose is to experience what is beyond this physical existence.

However, each one looks at life differently. Most human beings see life as a constant struggle for survival. Such people believe in the theory "the fittest will survive." They are satisfied with a normal way of living—for example, getting a house, a job, a car, a wife or husband, children and enough money to live. Yes, these are important things, and we need to focus on our day-to-day lives and to take care of our responsibilities and obligations, small and big. But there is more to life, a higher purpose, which is to know and realize who we are.

Questioner: Amma, what do we gain by knowing who we are?

Amma: Everything. A feeling of complete fullness, with absolutely nothing else to gain in life. That realization makes life perfect.

Regardless of all we have accumulated or are striving to acquire, for most people life still feels incomplete—like the letter "C." This gap, or lack, will always be there. Only spiritual knowledge and realization of the Self [Atman] can fill this gap and unite the two ends, which will make it like the letter "O." The knowledge of "That" alone will help us feel well-grounded in the real center of life.

Questioner: In that case, what about the worldly duties that people have to discharge?

Amma: No matter who we are or what we are doing, the duties we perform in the world should help us reach the supreme dharma, which is oneness with the Universal Self. All living beings are one because life is one, and life has only one purpose. Owing to identification with the body and mind, one may think, "To seek the Self and attain Self-realization is not my dharma; my dharma is to work as a musician or an actor or a businessman." It is okay if one feels this way. However, we will never find fulfillment unless we direct our energy toward the supreme goal of life.

Questioner: Amma, You say that for everyone the purpose of life is Self realization. But it doesn't seem like that, because most people don't attain realization or even seem to strive for it.

Amma: That is because most people have no spiritual understanding. That is what is known as *maya*, the illusory power of the world that covers Truth and distances humankind from it.

Whether we are aware of it or not, the real purpose of life is to realize the divinity within. There are many things you may not know in your present mental state. It is childish to say, "They are non-existent, because I am not aware of them." As situations and experiences unfold, new and unknown phases of life will open up, which will take you closer and closer to your own True Self. It is only a question of time. For some this realization may have already occurred; for certain others, it will happen any moment; and yet there are others who will realize it at a later stage. Just because it has not happened yet or may not even happen in this lifetime, don't think that it is never going to happen.

Within you, immense knowledge is waiting for your permission to unfold. But it won't happen unless you allow it to.

Questioner: Who should allow it? The mind?

Amma: Your whole being—your mind, body and intellect.

Questioner: Is it a question of understanding?

Amma: It is a question of understanding and doing.

Questioner: How do we develop that understanding?

Amma: By developing humility.

Questioner: What is so great about humility?

Amma: Humility makes you receptive to all experiences without judging them. So you learn more.

It is not a question of intellectual understanding alone. There are many people all over the world who have more than enough spiritual information in their heads. Yet among such people, how many are really spiritual and sincerely strive to attain the Goal or even try to gain a deeper understanding of spiritual principles? Very few, isn't it?

Questioner: So, Amma, what is the real problem? Is it faithlessness or the difficulty of getting out of our head?

Amma: If you have true faith, then you automatically fall into the heart.

Questioner: So, is it faithlessness?

Amma: What do you think?

Questioner: Yes, it is faithlessness. But why did You call it "falling" into the heart?

Amma: Physically speaking, the head is the topmost part of the body. To go from there to the heart, one must fall. However, spiritually speaking, it is rising up and soaring high.

Be Patient Because
You Are a Patient

Questioner: How does one get real help from a *Satguru* [True Master]?

Amma: To receive help, first accept that you are a patient and then be patient.

Questioner: Amma, are You our doctor?

Amma: No good doctor will walk around announcing, "I am the best doctor. Come to me. I will cure you." Even if a patient has the best doctor, unless the patient has faith in him or her, the treatment may not be very effective.

Irrespective of time and place, all surgeries that happen in life's operation theater are performed by God. You have seen how surgeons wear a mask while performing an operation. Nobody recognizes them at that time. But just behind the mask, it is the doctor. Likewise, just beneath the surface of all experiences in life is God's, or the Guru's, compassionate face.

Questioner: Amma, are You unsympathetic to Your disciples when it comes to removing their ego?

Amma: When a doctor operates and removes the cancerous part of a patient's body, do you interpret it as unsympathetic? If so, Amma too is unsympathetic, so to speak. But only if the children cooperate will She touch their ego.

Questioner: What do You do to help them?

Amma: Amma helps Her children see the cancer of the ego—the inner weaknesses and the negativities—and makes it easier for them to get rid of it. That is true compassion.

Questioner: Do You consider them as Your patients?

Amma: It is more important that *they* realize they are patients.

Questioner: Amma, what do you mean by "disciple's cooperation"?

Amma: Faith and love.

Questioner: Amma, this is a stupid question. But I cannot help asking it. Please forgive me if I am being too silly.

Amma: Go ahead and ask.

Questioner: What is the percentage of success in Your operations?

Amma laughed aloud and gently hit the top of the devotee's head.

Amma: (still laughing) Son, successful operations are very rare.

Questioner: Why?

Amma: Because the ego doesn't permit most people to cooperate with the doctor. It doesn't let the doctor do a good job.

Questioner: (mischievously) The doctor is You, isn't it?

Amma: (in English) I don't know.

Questioner: Okay, Amma, what is the basic requirement for such a surgery to become successful?

Amma: Once a patient is on the operating table, the only thing that he or she can do is to be still, have faith in the doctor and surrender. Nowadays, even for small operations, doctors give anesthesia to the patients. Nobody wants to experience pain. People would rather be unconscious than remain awake when they go through pain. Anesthesia, whether it is local or major, makes the patient unaware of the procedure. However, when a True Master works on you—on your ego—he or she prefers to do it while you are conscious. The Divine Master's surgery removes the disciple's cancerous ego. The whole process is much easier if the disciple can remain open and conscious.

The Real Meaning of Dharma

Questioner: Dharma is explained in different ways by different people. It is confusing to have so many interpretations for one single term such as dharma. Amma, what is the real meaning of dharma?

Amma: The real meaning of dharma dawns only when we experience God as our source and support. You cannot find it in words or books.

Questioner: That is the ultimate dharma, isn't it? But how can we find a meaning that fits our day-to-day life?

Amma: It is a revelation that occurs to each of us as we go through life's various experiences. For some people, this revelation comes fast. They find the right path and the right course of action in no time. For others, it is a slow process. They may have to go through a process of trial-and-error before they arrive at a spot in life from where they can start performing their dharma in this world. This doesn't mean that whatever they have done in the past has gone to waste. No, that will enrich their experience, and they will also learn a number of lessons from that, provided they remain open.

Questioner: Can leading a normal family life, facing the challenges and problems of a householder, obstruct one's spiritual awakening?

Amma: Not if we keep Self-realization as our final goal in life. If this is our goal, we will shape all our thoughts and actions in a way that will help us attain it, won't we? We will always be aware of our true destination. Someone traveling from one place to another may get down in several stops to have a cup of tea or to eat, but he or she will always return to the vehicle. Even while taking such small breaks they will be aware of their original destination. Likewise, in life, we may stop many times and do various things. However we musn't forget to re-board the vehicle carrying us along the spiritual path and to remain seated with our seatbelt tightly fastened.

Question: "Seatbelt tightly fastened"?

Amma: Yes. When you are flying, air pockets can create turbulence, and the ride can sometimes be bumpy. Even when traveling by road, accidents can occur. So it is always best to be safe and take certain security measures. Similarly, on the spiritual journey, situations that can cause mental and emotional turmoil cannot be ruled out. In order to safeguard ourselves from such circumstances, we must listen to the *Satguru* [True Master], and observe discipline and the dos and don'ts in life. Those are the seatbelts as far as the spiritual journey is concerned.

Question: So, whatever work we perform, it should not distract us from our ultimate dharma, which is God-realization. Amma, is this what You are suggesting?

Amma: Yes. For those of you who want to lead a life of contemplation and meditation, this fire of longing should remain ablaze within.

The meaning of dharma is "that which supports"—that which supports life and existence is the Atman [Self]. So, dharma, though commonly used to mean "one's duty" or the path that a person should pursue in the world, ultimately points to Self-realization. In this sense, only thoughts and actions that support our spiritual evolution can be called dharma.

Actions performed at the right time, with the right attitude, in the right way are dharmic. This sense of right action can help in the process of mental purification. You can be a businessman or a car driver, a butcher or a politician; whatever your job may be, if you perform your work as your dharma, as a means to *moksha* [liberation], then your actions become sacred. That is how the *gopis* [wives of the cow-herders] of Vrindavan, who earned their livelihood by selling milk and butter, became so close to God and finally attained the goal of life.

Love & love

Questioner: Amma, what is the difference between love and Love?

Amma: The difference between love and Love is the difference between human beings and God. Love is God's nature, and love is the nature of human beings.

Questioner: But Love is the true nature of human beings as well, isn't it so?

Amma: Yes, if one realizes that truth.

Consciousness & Awareness

uestioner: Amma, what is God?

Amma: God is pure consciousness; God is pure awareness.

Questioner: Are consciousness and awareness the same?

Amma: Yes, they are the same. The more aware you are, the more conscious you are and vice versa.

Questioner: Amma, what is the difference between matter and consciousness?

Amma: One is the outside and the other is the inside. The external is matter and the internal is consciousness. The outside is changing, and the inside, the indwelling Atman [Self], is changeless. It is the presence of the Atman that enlivens and illumines everything. The Atman is self-luminous, whereas matter is not. Without consciousness, matter remains unknown. However, once you transcend all differences, you see everything as pervaded with pure consciousness.

Questioner: "Beyond all differences," "everything is pervaded with pure consciousness"—Amma, You always use beautiful examples. Can You give one such example to make this point more visual?

Amma: (smiling) Thousands of such beautiful examples won't stop the mind from repeating the same questions. Only pure experience will clear all doubts. However, if the intellect gets a little more satisfaction from an example, Amma is not against it.

It is like being in a forest. When you are in the forest, you see all the different kinds of trees, plants and creepers in all their diversity. But when you step outside of the forest and start walking away from it, looking back, all the different trees and plants gradually disappear, until at last you behold everything as one forest. Likewise, as you transcend the mind, its limitations in the form of petty desires and all the differences created by the feelings of "I" and "you" will disappear. Then you will begin to experience everything as the one and only Self.

Consciousness Always Is

Questioner: If consciousness is always present, is there convincing proof of its existence?

Amma: Your own existence is the most convincing proof of consciousness. Can you deny your own existence? No, because even your denial is proof that you exist, isn't it? Suppose somebody asks, "Hey, are you there?" You reply, "No, I am not." Even the negative answer becomes clear evidence that you are very much there. You don't need to assert it. Just reject it and it is proved. So, the Atman [Self] cannot even be doubted.

Questioner: If so, why is the experience so difficult to attain?

Amma: "That which is" can only be experienced when we are aware of it. Otherwise it remains unknown to us, even though it exists. It is just that the truth of what is there was unknown to us. The law of gravity existed before it was discovered. A stone thrown upward has always had to come down again. In the same way, consciousness is always present within us—now, in the present moment—but we may not be aware of it. In fact, only the present moment is real. But to experience this, we need a new vision, a new eye and even a new body.

Questioner: "A new body"? What do You mean by that?

Amma: It doesn't mean that the body you have will disappear. It will look the same, but it will undergo a subtle change, a transformation. Because only then can it contain the ever-expanding consciousness.

Questioner: What do you mean by expanding consciousness? The Upanishads declare that the Absolute is *purnam* [ever-full]. The *Upanishads* say, "*purnamada purnamidam...*" ["This is the whole, that is the whole..."], so I don't understand how the already-perfect consciousness can grow?

Amma: That is very much true. However, on the individual or physical plane, the spiritual aspirant goes through an experience of expanding consciousness. The total *shakti* [divine energy], of course, is unchangeable. Though from the Vedantic [pertaining to the Hindu spiritual philosophy of non-dualism] point of view there is no spiritual journey, for the individual there is one such so-called journey toward the state of perfection. Once you attain the Goal, you will also realize that the whole process, including the journey, was unreal, because you were always there, in that state, never away from it. Until that final realization occurs, there is an expansion of awareness and consciousness depending on the progress of the *sadhak* [spiritual aspirant].

For example, what happens when you draw water from a well? The well is immediately replenished by the water from the spring beneath it. The spring will keep on filling the well. The more water you draw, the more water comes from the spring. So you could say that the water in the well keeps growing. The spring is a never-ending source. The well is full, and it remains full because it is eternally connected to the spring. The well keeps on becoming perfect. It keeps expanding.

Questioner: (after a thoughtful silence) It's very vivid, but still sounds complicated.

Amma: Yes, the mind will not understand it. Amma knows that. The easiest is the most difficult. The simplest remains the most complex. And the closest seems to be the farthest. It will continue to be a puzzle until you realize the Self. That is why the *Rishis* [ancient Seers] described the Atman as "farther than the farthest and nearer than the nearest."

Children, the human body is a very limited instrument. It cannot contain the unlimited consciousness. However, like the well, once we are connected to the eternal source of shakti, our consciousness will keep expanding within us. Once the state of ultimate *samadhi* [natural state of abidance] is reached, the connection between the body and the mind, between God and the world, will start functioning in perfect harmony. Thus, there is no growth, nothing. You remain one with the infinite ocean of consciousness.

No Claims

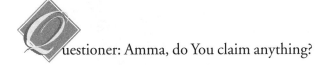

Questioner: Amma, do You claim anything?

Amma: Claim what?

Questioner: That You are an incarnation of the Divine Mother or a fully Self-realized Master and so forth.

Amma: Does the president or prime minister of any country keep on announcing, "Do you know who I am? I am the president/prime minister," wherever he or she goes? No. They are what they are. Even to claim that you are an Avatar [God descended in human form] or are Self-realized involves ego. In fact, if somebody claims that they are an Incarnation, a Perfect Soul, that in itself is proof that they are not.

Perfect Masters have no such claims. They always set an example to the world by being humble. Remember, Self-realization doesn't make you special. It makes you humble.

In order to claim that you are something, you neither have to be Self-realized nor do you need any special skill. The only thing that you have to have is a big ego, false pride. That is what a Perfect Master doesn't have.

Importance of the Guru
on the Spiritual Path

Questioner: Why is it that the Guru is given so much importance in the spiritual path?

Amma: Come on, tell Amma, is there any path or work that you can learn without the help of a teacher or guide? If you want to learn how to drive, you need to be taught by an experienced driver. A child needs to be taught how to tie his shoelaces. And how can you learn mathematics without a teacher? Even a pickpocket needs a teacher to teach him the art of stealing. If teachers are indispensable in ordinary life, wouldn't there be even more need of a teacher on the spiritual path, which is so extremely subtle?

If you want to go to a distant place, you may want to buy a map. But no matter how well you study the map, if you are heading toward a totally strange land, an unknown place, you won't know anything about that place until you actually arrive. Nor will the map tell you much about the journey itself, about the ups and downs of the road and the possible dangers on the way. It is therefore better to receive guidance from someone who has completed the journey, someone who knows the way from his or her own experience.

What do you know about the spiritual path? It is a totally unknown world and path. You may have collected some information from books or people. But when it comes to actually doing it, the experience part of it, a *Satguru*'s [True Master] direction is absolutely necessary.

Amma's Healing Touch

One day, a coordinator for Amma's European tours brought a young woman to Amma. The woman was crying profusely. "She has a very sad story to tell Amma," he told me. With tears coursing down her face, the woman told Amma that her father had left home when she was only five years old. As a little girl, she used to ask her mother about his whereabouts. But her mother never had anything good to say about the girl's father, because their relationship had been very bad. As the years went by, the young woman's curiosity about her father gradually died down.

Two years ago—that is 20 years after the disappearance of her father—the young woman's mother died. While going through her mother's belongings, she was amazed to find her father's address in one of her mother's old diaries. Soon she succeeded in getting his phone number. Unable to contain her excitement, she immediately called him. The joy of the father and daughter knew no bounds. After speaking for a long time over the phone, they decided to meet each other. He agreed to drive to the village where she lived, and a day was decided upon. But fate was extremely cruel, utterly ruthless. On the father's way to meet his daughter, an accident claimed his life.

The young woman was heartbroken. The hospital authorities summoned her to identify her father, and his body was handed over to her care. Imagine the devastated mental state of the young lady. She had been waiting with tremendous anticipation to see her father, whom she hadn't seen for 20 years, and then, finally, all she got to see of him was his dead body! To make things worse, the doctors told the young woman that the accident happened because her father had a heart attack while driving. Possibly this was due to his excitement over the idea of seeing his daughter after so many years.

That morning, while Amma received the young woman, I witnessed one of the most beautiful and touching darshans I have ever seen. As the woman cried her heart out, Amma wiped Her own tears, which streamed down Her face. Tenderly hugging the woman, Amma held her head in Her lap, wiped her tears, caressed and kissed her, affectionately saying to her, "My daughter, my child, don't cry!" Amma made the woman feel calm and comforted. There was almost no verbal communication between them. Observing this scene as openly as I could, I was learning another important lesson about the healing of a wounded heart, and how it happens in Amma's presence. There was an obvious change in the woman when she left. She seemed greatly relieved and relaxed. As she was about to walk away, she turned to me and said, "Having met Amma, I feel as light as a flower."

Amma uses very few words during such intense occasions, especially when it comes to sharing the pain and sorrow of others. Only silence coupled with deep feeling can reflect the pain of others. When such situations arise, Amma speaks through Her eyes, sharing Her child's pain and expressing Her deep love, concern, participation and caring.

As Amma says, "The ego cannot heal anyone. Talking high philosophy in a fancy language will only confuse people. On the other hand, a look or a touch of an egoless person will easily lift the clouds of pain and despair from one's mind. This is what leads to true healing."

Pain of Death

Questioner: Amma, why is there so much fear and pain associated with death?

Amma: Too much attachment to the body and the world creates pain and fear of death. Almost everyone believes that death is complete annihilation. No one wants to leave the world and disappear into oblivion. When we have such attachment, the process of letting go of the body and the world can be painful.

Questioner: Will death be painless if we outgrow that attachment?

Amma: If one transcends attachment to the body, not only will death become painless, it will become a blissful experience. You can remain a witness to the death of the body. A detached attitude makes death an entirely different experience.

The majority of people die in terrible disappointment and frustration. Consumed in deep sadness, they spend their last days in anxiety, pain and utter despair. Why? Because they never learned how to let go of, and free themselves from, their meaningless dreams, desires and attachments. Old age, especially the last days of such people, will become worse than hell. That is why wisdom is important.

Questioner: Will wisdom arise as one gets older?

Amma: That is the common belief. Having seen and experienced all while going through the different phases of life, wisdom is supposed to dawn. However, it is not so easy to attain that level of wisdom, particularly in today's world, where people have become so self-centered.

Questioner: What is the basic quality that one needs to develop for gaining that kind of wisdom?

Amma: A contemplative and meditative life. This gives us the capacity to go deeper into the various experiences of life.

Questioner: Amma, as the majority of people in the world are neither contemplative nor meditative in nature, is this really practical for them?

Amma: It depends on how much importance one attaches to it. Remember, there was a time when contemplation and meditation were part and parcel of life. That is why so much could be achieved then even though science and technology were not as developed as they are today. The findings of those days continue to be the basis for what we do in modern times.

In today's world, what is most important is often not accepted, being declared as "impractical." This is one of the characteristics of Kaliyuga, the age of materialistic darkness. It is easy to awaken a person who is sleeping, but difficult to awaken somebody who is pretending to be sleeping. Is there any use in holding a mirror in front of a blind person? In this age, people prefer to keep their eyes closed to Truth.

Questioner: Amma, what is true wisdom?

Amma: That which helps make life simple and beautiful is true wisdom. It is the right understanding that one gains through proper discrimination. When one has truly imbibed this quality, it will be reflected in one's thoughts and actions.

Humanity at Present

Questioner: What is the spiritual state of humanity at present?

Amma: Generally speaking, there is tremendous spiritual awakening throughout the world. People are certainly becoming more and more aware of the need for a spiritual way of living. Though they don't directly link it with spirituality, New Age philosophy, yoga and meditation are gaining more popularity in Western countries than ever before. To do yoga and meditation has become fashionable in many countries, especially in the higher class of society. The basic idea of living in tune with Nature and with spiritual principles is being accepted even by atheists. An inner thirst and a feeling of urgency to change can be found everywhere. This is undoubtedly a positive sign.

However, on the other hand, the influence of materialism and materialistic pleasures are also increasing uncontrollably. If things continue in this way, it will cause serious imbalance. When it comes to material pleasures, people use very poor discrimination and their approach is often unintelligent and destructive.

Question: Is there anything new or special about this age?

Amma: Every moment is special, so to speak. Nevertheless, this age is special, because we have almost reached another peak of human existence.

Question: Really? What is that peak?

Amma: The peak of ego, darkness and selfishness.

Question: Amma, would You please elaborate a little more on that?

Amma: According to the Rishis [ancient Seers], there are four ages: Satyayuga, Tretayuga, Dwaparayuga and Kaliyuga. Presently we are in Kaliyuga, the dark age of materialism. Satyayuga comes first, a time when only truth and truthfulness exist. Having journeyed through the other two, Treta and Dwapara yugas, humanity has now reached Kaliyuga, the last one, which is supposed to culminate into another Satyayuga. However, as we entered, sojourned and came out of the Treta and Dwapara yugas, we also lost many beautiful values, such as truth, compassion, love, etc. The age of truth and truthfulness was a peak. Treta and Dwapara yugas were the middle, when we still maintained a little bit of dharma [righteousness] and *satya* [truth]. Now, we have reached another peak, the peak of *adharma* [unrighteousness] and *asatya* [untruthfulness]. Lessons in humility alone will help humanity to realize the darkness that currently surrounds it. This will prepare us to climb to the top of light and truthfulness. Let us hope and pray that people belonging to all faiths and all cultures around the world learn this lesson, which is the need of the age.

Shortcut to Self-Realization

Questioner: In today's world, people seek short cuts to all gains. Is there any short cut to Self-realization?

Amma: The question is like asking, "Is there any shortcut to myself?" Self-realization is the path to your own Self. So, it is as simple as turning on a light switch. However, you should know which switch to press and how, because this switch is hidden inside yourself. You cannot find it anywhere outside. That is where you need the help of a Divine Master.

The door is always open. You only have to walk through.

To Progress Spiritually

Questioner: Amma, I have been meditating for many years now. However, I don't think I'm really progressing. Am I doing something wrong? Do you think I am doing the right spiritual practices?

Amma: First of all, Amma wants to know why you think you are not progressing. What is your criterion for spiritual progress?

Questioner: I've never had any visions.

Amma: What kind visions do you expect?

Questioner: I've never seen any divine blue light.

Amma: Where did you get the idea of seeing a blue light?

Questioner: One of my friends told me. I have also read it in books.

Amma: Son, don't have unnecessary ideas about your *sadhana* [spiritual practices] and spiritual growth. This is what is wrong. Your ideas about spirituality in themselves can become stumbling blocks in your path. You are doing the right sadhana, but your attitude is wrong. You are waiting for the divine blue light to appear in front of you. The strange thing is that you have absolutely no idea what divine light is, yet you think it is blue. Who knows, it might have already appeared, but you were waiting for a particular divine blue light. What if divinity decided to appear as a red or green light? Then you might have missed it.

There was one son who once told Amma that he was waiting for a green light to appear in his meditations. So Amma told him to be careful while driving, as he might go through red lights, thinking that they are green. Such concepts about spirituality are really dangerous.

Son, experiencing peace in all circumstances is the goal of all spiritual practices. Everything else—whether it is light, sound or form—will come and go. Even if you have some visions, they will be temporary. The only permanent experience is complete peace. That peace and the experience of evenness of mind, indeed, is the true fruit of spiritual life.

Questioner: Amma, is it wrong to desire such experiences?

Amma: Amma wouldn't say it is wrong. Nevertheless, don't give too much importance to them, as doing so can really slow down your spiritual growth. If they occur, let it be. That is the right attitude.

In the beginning stages of spiritual life, a seeker will have a lot of misconceptions and wrong notions about spirituality due to over-excitement and low awareness. For example, some people are crazy for visions of gods and goddesses. Longing to see different colors is yet another craving. Beautiful sounds are an attraction for many people. How many people waste their entire life running after *siddhis* [yogic powers]! There are also people who are eager to get instant *samadhi* [state of natural abidance] and *moksha* [liberation]. People have heard so many stories about *kundalini* [spiritual energy laying dormant in the base of the spine] awakening as well. A true spiritual seeker will never be obsessed with such ideas. These concepts can very well slow down our spiritual progress. That is why it is important to have a clear understanding and a healthy, intelligent approach to one's spiritual life from the very beginning. Indiscriminately listening to whoever claims to be a Master and reading books without being selective adds to the confusion.

The Mind of a Self-Realized Soul

Questioner: What is the mind of a Self-realized soul?

Amma: It is a mindless mind.

Questioner: Is it no mind?

Amma: It is expansiveness.

Questioner: But they too interact with the world. How is this possible without a mind?

Amma: Of course, they "use" the mind for interacting with the world. However, there is a big difference between the common human mind, which is full of various thoughts, and the mind of a Mahatma. Mahatmas use the mind, and we are used by the mind. They are not calculative, but spontaneous. Spontaneity is the nature of the heart. A person who is overly identified with the mind cannot be spontaneous.

Questioner: The majority of people who live in the world are identified with their minds. Are You saying that all of them are manipulative in nature?

Amma: No, there are plenty of occasions when people identify with the heart and its positive feelings. When people are kind, compassionate and considerate to others, they dwell more in their heart than in their mind. But are they always able to behave so? No, so more often people are identified with the mind. That is what Amma meant.

Questioner: If the capacity to remain perfectly in tune with the positive feelings of the heart is dormant in everyone, why doesn't it happen more often?

Amma: Because, in your present state, the mind is more powerful. In order to remain attuned with the positive feelings of the heart, you should strengthen your connection with the silence of your spiritual heart and weaken your connection with the disturbances of your noisy mind.

Questioner: What enables a person to be spontaneous and open?

Amma: Less interference of ego.

Questioner: What happens when there is less interference of ego?

Amma: You will be overpowered by an intense longing from deep within. Though you have prepared the ground for that to happen, there won't be any calculative move or effort when it actually takes place. That action, or whatever it may be, becomes so beautiful and fulfilling. Others too will be very attracted to what you have done at that time. Such moments are more the expressions of your heart. At that time you are closer to your true being.

In reality such moments come from the beyond—beyond the mind and intellect. A sudden tuning with Infinity takes place, and you tap into the source of universal energy.

Perfect Masters always dwell in this state of spontaneity, and they create the same situation for others as well.

Distance Between Amma and Us

Questioner: Amma, what is the distance between us and You?

Amma: Nothing and infinite.

Questioner: Nothing and infinite?

Amma: Yes, there is absolutely no distance between you and Amma. But at the same time, the distance is infinite as well.

Questioner: That sounds contradictory.

Amma: The limitations of the mind make it sound contradictory. It will continue to be like that until you attain the final state of realization. No explanation, no matter how intelligent or logical it may sound, will remove that contradiction.

Questioner: I understand the limitations of my mind. Still, I don't understand why it should be so paradoxical and ambiguous. How can it be nothing and infinite at the same time?

Amma: First of all, daughter, you haven't understood the limitations of your mind. To really understand the smallness of the mind is to really understand the bigness of God, the divine. The mind is a big burden. Once true understanding of this dawns, you will realize the pointlessness of carrying this huge load called the mind. You cannot carry it any longer. That realization helps you to drop it.

Daughter, as long as you remain ignorant about the inner divinity, the distance is infinite. However, the moment enlightenment dawns, the realization that there never was any distance also takes place.

Questioner: It is impossible for the intellect to understand the whole process.

Amma: Daughter, that is a good sign. At least, you agree that it is not possible for the intellect to understand the so-called process.

Questioner: Does that mean there is no such process?

Amma: Exactly. For example, there is a man who was born blind. Does he have any knowledge about light? No, the poor man is only familiar with darkness, an entirely different world compared to that of those blessed with sight.

The doctor tells him, "Look, your eyesight can be restored if you undergo a surgery. Some correction is needed."

If the man opts for the surgery as instructed by the doctor, darkness will soon disappear and light will appear, won't it? Now, where does the light come from, somewhere outside? No, the seer was always waiting right inside the man. Likewise, when you correct your inner vision through spiritual practices, the already-waiting light of pure knowledge will dawn within.

Amma's Ways

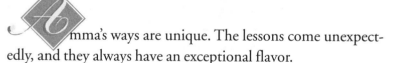

mma's ways are unique. The lessons come unexpectedly, and they always have an exceptional flavor.

During the morning *darshan*, one retreat registrant brought another woman who was not part of the retreat. I noticed the newcomer and informed Amma. But Amma completely ignored me and continued giving darshan.

I thought, "That is fine; Amma is busy. However, let me keep an eye on the gatecrasher." So, for the next few minutes, though my main *seva* [selfless service] was translating the devotees' questions to Amma, I chose as my subsidiary seva the close observation of every movement of the non-registrant. She remained glued to the devotee who had brought her, so my eyes closely followed wherever they went. Simultaneously, I was giving Amma a running commentary on their movements. Though Amma wasn't listening to me, I considered it my duty to do so anyway.

As soon as they both joined the Special Needs line, I enthusiastically brought it to Amma's attention. However, Amma continued giving darshan to the devotees.

Meanwhile, a couple of devotees joined my side. Pointing to the "encroacher," one of them said, "See that lady? She is weird. I heard her talk. She is very negative. I don't think it is wise to keep her inside the hall."

The other devotee seriously inquired, "Ask Amma what we should do about her—kick her out?"

After much effort, I succeeded in getting Amma's attention. She finally looked up and asked, "Where is she?"

All three of us were overjoyed. We thought—at least, I thought—that Amma would soon utter those most pleasing three words that we were impatiently waiting to hear: "Throw her out."

Hearing Amma ask, "Where is she?" all three of us pointed to the place where the non-registrant lady was sitting. Amma looked at her. Now, we were anxiously waiting for the final judgment. Amma turned toward us and said, "Call her." We were almost falling over each other to summon the lady.

As soon as the lady was near the darshan chair, Amma stretched out Her arms and, with a benign smile on Her face, said, "Come, my daughter." The stranger spontaneously fell into Amma's arms. As we were watching, the lady had one of the most beautiful darshans. Amma tenderly put the woman on Her shoulder and gently stroked her back. Then, holding the lady's face in Her cupped hands, Amma looked deep into her eyes. Tears rolled down the lady's cheeks, and Amma compassionately wiped them with Her hands.

Unable to control our tears, my two "colleagues" and I stood behind the darshan chair in a completely softened mood.

As soon as the lady left, Amma looked at me and, with a smile on Her face, said, "You wasted so much of your energy this morning."

Awestruck, I looked at the small figure of Amma, as She continued showering bliss and blessings on Her children. Though tongue tied, I remembered a beautiful saying of Amma's at that moment: "Amma is like a river. She simply flows. Some people take a bath in the river. Others quench their thirst by drinking its water. There are people who come to swim and enjoy its water. Yet, there are people who spit in it. Whatever happens, the river accepts everything and flows unaffected, embracing all that come to its fold."

Thus I had another amazing moment in the presence of Amma, the Supreme Master.

No New Truth

Questioner: Amma, do You think that humanity needs a new truth to awaken it?

Amma: Humanity doesn't need a new truth. What is required is to see the already existing Truth. There is only one Truth. That Truth always shines within all of us. That one and only Truth can neither be new, nor can it be old. It is always the same, unchangeable, ever new. Asking for a new Truth is like a pre-primary student asking the teacher, "Miss, you have been telling us that 2+2 is 4 for such a long time. It has become so old. Why can't you say something new, like that it is 5 instead of 4 all the time?" Truth cannot be changed. It has always been there and has always been the same.

This new millennium will see a lot of spiritual awakening, both in the East and the West. That, indeed, is the need of the age. The increasing amount of scientific knowledge that humanity has acquired must lead us to God.

Truth

uestion: Amma, what is Truth?

Amma: Truth is that which is eternal and unchangeable.

Questioner: Is truthfulness Truth?

Amma: Truthfulness is only a quality, not Truth the ultimate reality.

Questioner: Isn't that quality part of Truth the ultimate reality?

Amma: Yes, just as everything is part of Truth the ultimate reality, truthfulness, too, is part of it.

Questioner: If everything is part of the ultimate reality, then not only good qualities, but bad qualities are also part of it, aren't they?

Amma: Yes, but daughter, you are still on earth and have not reached those heights.

Suppose you are going to fly in a plane for the first time. Until you board the aircraft, you won't have any idea about flying. You look around and you see people; they're talking and shouting. There are buildings, trees, vehicles moving about, the sounds of children crying and so forth. After some time you get on the plane. Then the flight takes off, and it slowly flies higher and higher. At that point, when you look down, you see everything becoming smaller and smaller, gradually disappearing into oneness. At last, everything disappears and you are surrounded by vast space.

Likewise, child, you are still on the earth and have not yet boarded the flight. You have to accept, imbibe and practice good qualities, and reject the bad qualities. Once you reach the heights of realization, then you experience everything as One.

One-Sentence Piece of Advice

Questioner: Amma, can You give me a one-sentence piece of advice for my peace of mind?

Amma: Permanent or temporary?

Questioner: Permanent, of course.

Amma: Then, find your Self [the Atman].

Questioner: That is too difficult to understand.

Amma: Okay, then love all.

Questioner: Are they two different answers?

Amma: No, only the words are different. Finding one's Self and loving everyone equally are basically the same thing; they are interdependent. (laughing) Son, it is already more than one sentence.

Questioner: Sorry, Amma. I am stupid.

Amma: That is okay; don't worry. But do you want to continue?

Questioner: Yes, Amma. Do peace, love and true happiness develop along with our *sadhana* [spiritual practices]? Or are they only the end result?

Amma: Both. However, only when we rediscover the Inner Self will the circle become complete and will perfect peace ensue.

Questioner: What do you mean by "the circle"?

Amma: The circle of our inner and outer existence, the state of perfection.

Questioner: But the scriptures say that it is already complete, a circle. If it is already a circle, then what is the question of completing it?

Amma: Of course, it is a perfect circle. But most people don't realize this. For them, there is a gap to be filled. And it is in attempt to fill this gap that every human being runs around in the name of various needs, demands and desires.

Questioner: Amma, I have heard that in the state of supreme realization there is no such thing as inner and outer existence.

Amma: Yes, but that is only the experience of those who are established in that state.

Questioner: Will understanding that state intellectually help?

Amma: Help what?

Questioner: Help me to get a glimpse of that state.

Amma: No, an intellectual understanding will only gratify the intellect. And even that satisfaction is only temporary. You may think that you've understood it, but soon you will have doubts and questions again. Your understanding is based only on limited words and explanations; they cannot give you the experience of the unlimited.

Questioner: So, what is the best way?

Amma: Work hard until surrender happens.

Questioner: What do You mean by "work hard"?

Amma: Amma means patiently do *tapas* [austerities]. Only if you do tapas, will you be able to remain in the present.

Questioner: Is tapas sitting continuously and performing long hours of meditation?

Amma: That is only part of it. Carrying out every action and thought in a way so that it helps us to become one with God, or the Self, is real tapas.

Questioner: What is it exactly?

Amma: It is your life offered to the goal of God-realization.

Questioner: I am a little confused.

Amma: (smiling) Not a little—you are very confused.

Questioner: You are right. But why?

Amma: Because you are thinking too much about spirituality and the state beyond the mind. Stop thinking and use that energy to do what you can. That will give you the experience—or at least a glimpse—of that reality.

Need for a Time Table

Questioner: Amma, You say that one must keep a daily discipline, like a timetable and stick to it as much as possible. However, Amma, I am the mother of a little baby. What if my child cries when I am about to meditate?

Amma: It is very simple. Take care of the baby first and then meditate. If you choose to meditate without paying attention to the child, then you will only be meditating on the child, not on the Self, or God.

Following a timetable will certainly be beneficial in the beginning stages. Also a true *sadhak* [spiritual seeker] should exercise control all the time, throughout the day and night.

Some people have the habit of drinking coffee as soon as they get up. If one day they don't get it on time, they will feel so uneasy. It may even spoil their whole day, causing stomachache, constipation and headache. In a similar manner, meditation, prayer and chanting mantra should also become part and parcel of a sadhak's life. If you ever miss it, you should be able to feel it deeply. From that, the longing to never miss it should arise.

Self-Effort

Questioner: Amma, some people say that because our real nature is the Atman, it is not necessary to perform spiritual practices. They say, "I am That, the absolute consciousness, so what is the point in performing *sadhana* [spiritual practices], if I am already That?" Do you think such people are authentic?

Amma: Amma doesn't want to say whether these people are authentic or inauthentic. However, Amma feels such people are either pretending to be like that, or they are totally deluded, or they are lazy. Amma wonders if these people would say, "I don't need to eat or drink because I am not the body"?

Suppose, they are brought into the dining room, with a number of plates nicely arranged on the table, but where there is supposed to be a sumptuous meal, there is only a piece of paper on which is written "rice," another reading "steamed vegetables," "sweet pudding" and so on. Will these people be willing to imagine that they have eaten to their heart's content and that their hunger is completely appeased?

The tree is potent in the seed. However, what if the seed egoistically feels, "I don't want to bow down to this earth. I am the tree. I needn't go beneath this dirty soil." If that is the seed's attitude, it simply won't sprout, the seedling won't come out and it will never become a tree, providing shade and fruit for others. Just because the seed thinks that it is a tree, nothing will happen. It will continue to be a seed. So, be a seed but have the willingness to fall to the earth and go beneath the soil. Then the earth will take care of the seed.

Grace

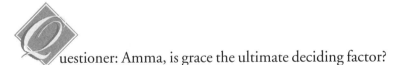

Questioner: Amma, is grace the ultimate deciding factor?

Amma: Grace is the factor that brings the right result at the right time in the right proportion to your actions.

Questioner: Even if you completely dedicate yourself to your work, will the result depend on how much grace you have?

Amma: Dedication is the most essential aspect. The more dedicated you are, the more open you remain. The more open you are, the more love you experience. The more love you have, the more grace you experience.

Grace is openness. It is the spiritual strength and the intuitive vision that you can experience while performing an action. By remaining open to a particular situation, you are letting go of your ego and narrow-minded views. This transforms your mind into a better channel through which *shakti* [divine energy] can flow. That flow of shakti and its expression through our actions is grace.

Someone may be a fantastic singer. But while performing on the stage, they should allow the shakti of music to flow through them. This brings grace along with it and helps them transport the entire audience.

Questioner: Where is the source of grace?

Amma: The real source of grace is within. However, as long you don't realize this, it will seem to remain somewhere far beyond.

Questioner: Beyond?

Amma: Beyond means the origin, which is unknown to you in your current mental state. When a singer sings from the heart, he or she is in touch with divinity, with beyond-ness. Where does the soul-stirring music come from? You may say from the throat or heart. But if you look inside, will you see it? No, so it comes from beyond. That source, indeed, is divinity. Once the final realization happens, you will find that source within.

Sannyas: Beyond Categorization

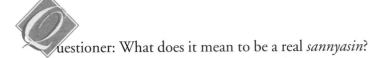

Questioner: What does it mean to be a real *sannyasin*?

Amma: A true sannyasin is one who has gone beyond all the limitations created by the mind. At present we are hypnotized by the mind. In the state of sannyas, we will become completely free from the grip of that hypnosis. We will wake up as though from a dream—like a drunk coming out of intoxication.

Questioner: Is sannyas also attaining Godhood?

Amma: Amma would rather put it this way: sannyas is a state where one is able to behold and adore the entire creation as God.

Questioner: Is humility a sign of a true sannyasin?

Amma: True sannyasins cannot be categorized. They are beyond. If you say such and such a person is very simple and humble, still there is "someone" who is feeling simple and humble. In the state of sannyas, that "someone," which is the ego, disappears. Normally, humility is the opposite of arrogance. Love is the opposite of hate. Whereas a real sannyasin is neither humble nor arrogant—he or she is neither love nor hate. One who has attained sannyas is beyond everything. He or she has nothing to gain or to lose anymore. When we call a genuine sannyasin "humble," it not only means absence of arrogance, but it signifies absence of ego as well.

Someone asked a Mahatma, "Who are you?"

"I am not," he replied.

"Are you God?"

"No, I am not."

"Are you a saint or a sage?"

"No, I am not."

"Are you an atheist?"

"No, I am not."

"Then who are you?"

"I am what I am. I am pure awareness."

Sannyas is the state of pure awareness.

A Divine Play in Mid-Air

Scene I: The Air India flight to Dubai has just taken off. The aircrew is preparing for the initial service of soft drinks. Suddenly, one by one, all the passengers get up from their seats and move in procession toward the Business Class Section. Not understanding what is happening, the startled crew requests everyone to take their seats. Finding it totally ineffective, they finally implore everyone to cooperate until they finish serving the food.

"We want to have Amma's *darshan!*" shout the passengers.

"We understand," replies the crew. "Just please bear with us until we finish serving."

The passengers eventually yield to the requests of the aircrew and go back to their seats.

Scene II: The serving is now finished. The airhostesses and host temporarily become the line monitors and control the darshan line, which sluggishly moves toward Amma's seat. Owing to short notice, no darshan tokens could be arranged. Regardless, the aircrew does a good job.

Scene III: Having received Amma's darshan, the passengers now look very happy and relaxed. They settle down in their respective seats. Now the entire crew, including the pilot and the co-pilot, begin queuing up. Of course they had been waiting for their turn. Each one gets a motherly hug. Along with that, they also receive Amma's whispers of love and grace, an unforgettable radiant smile and candy *prasad* [blessed gift] from Amma.

Scene IV: The same thing happens on the return flight.

Sympathy & Compassion

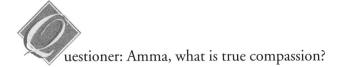

uestioner: Amma, what is true compassion?

Amma: True compassion is the ability to see and know what is beyond. Only those who have the capacity to see beyond can offer real help and uplift others.

Questioner: Beyond what?

Amma: Beyond the body and mind, beyond the outer appearance.

Questioner: So, Amma, what is the difference between sympathy and compassion?

Amma: Compassion is real help that you receive from a True Master. The Master sees beyond. Whereas sympathy is temporary help you receive from people around you. And sympathy cannot go beneath the surface and go beyond. Compassion is right understanding with a deeper knowledge of the person, the situation and what he or she truly needs. Sympathy is more superficial.

Questioner: How do you distinguish between the two?

Amma: It is hard. However, Amma will give you an example. It is not uncommon for surgeons to instruct their patients to get up and walk on the second or third day, even after major surgeries. If the patient is reluctant to do so, a good doctor, who knows the consequences, will always force the patient to get out of bed and walk. Seeing the pain and struggle of the patient, his relatives may comment, "What a cruel doctor! Why is he forcing him to walk when he doesn't want to? This is too much."

In this example, the attitude of the relatives can be called sympathy, and the attitude of the doctor, compassion. In this case, who is really helping the patient—the doctor or the relatives? If the patient thinks, "This doctor is useless. After all, who is he to give instructions? What does he know about me? So, let him talk his head off; I am not going to listen." Such an attitude will never help the patient.

Questioner: Can sympathy harm a person?

Amma: If we are not careful and offer our sympathy without understanding the subtle aspects of a particular situation and a person's mental constitution, it can be harmful. It is dangerous when people attach too much importance to sympathetic words.

It can even become an obsession, gradually ruining one's discriminative power by building a small cocoon-like world around them. They may feel comforted, but they might never put forth any effort to come out of their situation. Without their knowledge, they may move more and more into darkness.

Questioner: Amma, what do you mean by "cocoon-like world"?

Amma: Amma means you will lose your capacity to look deeper into yourself, to see what is really going on. You will give too much importance to the other person's words and trust him or her blindly without properly using your discrimination.

Sympathy is superficial love without any knowledge about the root cause of the problem. Whereas compassion is love that sees the real source of the problem and deals with it appropriately.

True Love Is the State of Complete Fearlessness

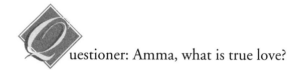

Questioner: Amma, what is true love?

Amma: True love is the state of complete fearlessness. Fear is part and parcel of the mind. Therefore, fear and genuine love cannot go together. As the depth of love increases, the intensity of fear slowly decreases.

Fear can exist only when you are identified with the body and mind. Transcending the weaknesses of the mind and living in love is Godliness. The more love you have, the more divinity is expressed within you. The less love you have, the more fear you have and the more you move away from the center of life. Fearlessness, indeed, is one of the greatest qualities of a true lover.

Do's & Don'ts

uestioner: Amma, cultivating purity and other moral values are considered to be important in spiritual life. However, there are New Age gurus who deny that this is necessary. Amma, what is Your opinion about this?

Amma: It is very much true that moral values play a significant role in spiritual life. Each path, whether it is spiritual or material, has certain do's and don'ts to follow. Unless the prescribed conditions are followed, attaining the desired result will be difficult. The subtler the ultimate fruit, the more intense the path to it will be. Spiritual realization is the subtlest of all experiences, therefore the rules and regulations it demands are rigorous.

A patient cannot eat and drink whatever he or she wants. Depending on the illness, there will be restrictions of diet and movement. If they are not observed, it can affect the healing process. The condition can even become aggravated if the patient doesn't adhere to the instructions. Is it wise if the patient asks, "Do I really have to observe these rules and regulations?" There are musicians who practice 18 hours a day in order to attain perfection on their instruments. Whatever is your area of interest—whether it is spirituality, science, politics, sports or arts—your success and ascension in that field solely depends on the way you approach it, the amount of time you sincerely spend in achieving your goal and how much you follow the essential required principles.

Questioner: So, is purity the basic quality required to reach the Goal?

Amma: It can be purity. It can be love, compassion, forgiveness, patience or perseverance. Just pick one quality and observe it with utmost faith and optimism; other qualities will automatically follow. The purpose is to go beyond the limitations of the mind.

Amma, an Offering to the World

Questioner: Amma, what do You expect from Your disciples?

Amma: Amma doesn't expect anything from anyone. Amma has offered Herself to the world. Once you become an offering, how can you expect anything from anyone? All expectations arise from the ego.

Questioner: But, Amma, You speak a lot about surrender to the Guru. Is that not an expectation?

Amma: True, Amma speaks about it, not because She expects surrender from Her children, but because that is the crux of spiritual life. The Guru offers everything that he or she has to the disciple. As a *Satguru* [Perfect Master] is a completely surrendered soul, that is what his or her presence offers and teaches the disciples. It happens spontaneously. Depending on the maturity and understanding of the disciple, he or she accepts it or rejects it. Whatever be the disciple's attitude, a Satguru will keep giving. He or she cannot do otherwise.

Questioner: What happens when a disciple surrenders to a Satguru?

Amma: Like a lamp lighted from the main lamp, the disciple will also become a light that guides the world. The disciple too becomes a Master.

Questioner: What helps the most in that process: the Master's form or his or her formless aspect?

Amma: Both. The formless consciousness inspires the disciple through the form of the Satguru as pure love, compassion and surrender.

Questioner: Is the disciple surrendering to the form of the Master or to the formless consciousness?

Amma: It begins as surrender to the physical form. However, it ends as surrender to the formless consciousness, which is when the disciple realizes his or her own True Self. Even in the initial stages of *sadhana* [spiritual practices], when the disciple surrenders to the Master's form, in reality he or she is surrendering to the formless consciousness, only the disciple is not aware of it.

Questioner: Why?

Amma: Because disciples only know the body; consciousness is completely unknown to them.

A true disciple will continue to worship the Guru's form as an expression of gratitude to the Guru showering his or her grace and showing him the path.

Satguru's Form

Questioner: Can you explain the nature of a *Satguru's* [True Master] physical form in a simple way?

Amma: A Satguru is both with and without form, like chocolate. The moment you put it in your mouth, it melts and becomes formless; it becomes a part of you. Likewise, when you truly imbibe the Master's teachings and make them part of your life, you will realize that the Master is the formless supreme consciousness.

Questioner: So, we should eat Amma up?

Amma: Yes, eat Amma if you can. She is very much willing to become food for your soul.

Questioner: Amma, thank You for the chocolate example. That made it very easy to understand, because I love chocolate.

Amma: (laughing) But don't fall in love with it, because it will be bad for your health.

Perfect Disciples

Questioner: What does one gain by becoming a perfect disciple?

Amma: Becoming a Perfect Master.

Questioner: How do You describe Yourself?

Amma: Definitely not as something.

Questioner: Then?

Amma: As nothingness.

Questioner: Does that mean as everything?

Amma: That means She is always present and available for everyone.

Questioner: Does "everyone" mean all those who come to You?

Amma: "Everyone" means whoever is open.

Questioner: Does that mean that Amma is not available for those who are not open?

Amma: Amma's physical presence is available for everyone, whether they accept Her or not. But the experience is only available to those who are open. The flower is there, but the beauty and fragrance will be experienced only by those who are open. A person with blocked nostrils cannot experience it. In a similar manner, closed hearts cannot experience what Amma is offering.

Vedanta & Creation

Questioner: Amma, there are some conflicting theories about creation. Those who follow the path of devotion say that God created the world, whereas Vedantins [non-dualists] are of the opinion that everything is a creation of the mind, and therefore it is only there as long as the mind exists. Which of these views is true?

Amma: Both views are correct. Whereas a devotee sees the Supreme Lord as the creator of the world, the Vedantin sees Brahman as the underlying principle that serves as the substratum of the changing world. For the Vedantin, the world is a projection of the mind; whereas for the devotee it is the *leela* [play] of his or her Beloved Lord. These may seem like two entirely different perspectives, but as you go deeper into it, you will find that they are basically the same.

Name and form are associated with the mind. When the mind ceases to exist, name and form also disappear. The world, or creation, consists of names and forms. A God, or a Creator, is significant only when creation exists. Even God has a name and a form. For the world of names and forms to come into existence, a corresponding cause is necessary—and that cause we call God.

True Vedanta is the highest form of knowledge. Amma is not talking about Vedanta in the form of scriptural texts or the Vedanta that so-called Vedantins talk about. Amma is talking about Vedanta as the supreme experience, as a way of living, as evenness of mind in all situations of life.

However, this is not easy. Unless a transformation happens, this experience will not dawn. It is this revolutionary change on the intellectual and emotional levels that makes the mind subtle, expansive and powerful. The more subtle and expansive the mind becomes, the more it becomes "no-mind." Gradually, the mind disappears. When there is no mind, where is God and where is the world or creation? Nevertheless, this doesn't mean that the world will disappear from your sight, but a transformation will happen and you will behold the One in the many.

Questioner: Does this mean that in that state God is also an illusion?

Amma: Yes, from the ultimate point of view, God with a form is an illusion. However, it depends on the depth of your inner experience. Nevertheless, is the attitude of the so-called Vedantins who egoistically feel that even the forms of the Gods and Goddesses are insignificant is incorrect. Remember, ego will never help in this path. Humbleness alone will.

Questioner: That part I understand. But Amma, You also mentioned that from the ultimate point of view, God with a form is an illusion. So are You saying that the different forms of the Gods and Goddesses are just projections of the mind?

Amma: Ultimately they are. Whatever will perish is not real. All forms, even those of the Gods and Goddesses, have a beginning and an end. That which is born and dies is mental; it is associated with the thought process. And whatever is associated with the mind is bound to change, because it exists in time. The only unchangeable truth is that which always remains, the substratum of the mind and intellect. That is the Atman [Self], the ultimate state of existence.

Questioner: If even the forms of the Gods and Goddesses are unreal, what is the point of building temples and worshipping them?

Amma: No, you do not understand the point. You cannot discard the Gods and Goddesses just like that. To people who are still identified with the mind, and who have not yet reached the highest state, those forms certainly are real and are very much needed for their spiritual growth. They help them tremendously.

The government in a country consists of several sections and departments. From the president or the prime minister downward, there are a number of ministers, and below them there are so many other officials and various other departments down to the attendants and sweepers.

Suppose you want to get something done. You will go directly to the president or the prime minister, provided you know them or have contact with them. This will make things much easier and smoother for you. Your need, whatever it may be, will be immediately taken care of. But the majority of people have no direct contact or influence. To get things done or to access the higher authorities, they have to stick to the normal course— contacting one of the junior officers or lower departments, sometimes even an attendant. Likewise, as long as we are in the physical plane of existence and identify with the mind and its thought patterns, we need to accept and recognize the different forms of divinity, until we establish a direct connection with the inner source of pure energy.

Questioner: But Vedantins usually don't agree with this perspective.

Amma: Which Vedantins are you talking about? A bookworm Vedantin who repeats the scriptures like a trained parrot or a tape recorder may not, but a true Vedantin definitely will. A Vedantin who doesn't accept the world and the path of devotion is not a true Vedantin. Accepting the world and recognizing the many but at the same time seeing the one Truth in the many is real Vedanta.

A Vedantin who considers the path of love to be inferior is neither a Vedantin nor a true spiritual seeker. True Vedantins cannot do their spiritual practices without love.

The form will take you to the formless, provided you do your spiritual practices with the proper attitude. *Saguna* [form] is *nirguna* [formless] manifested. If one doesn't understand this simple principle, what is the point of calling oneself a Vedantin?

Questioner: Amma, You said that a devotee sees the world as the leela of God. What does leela mean?

Amma: It is a one-word definition for supreme detachment. The ultimate state of *sakshi* [witnessing] without exercising any form of authority is known as leela. When we remain completely away from the mind and its various projections, how can we feel any attachment or feel any authority? Watching everything that happens inside and outside without getting involved is real fun, a beautiful play.

Questioner: We have heard that the reason Amma stopped manifesting Krishna Bhava* is because You were in that state of leela at that time?

Amma: That was one of the reasons. Krishna was detached. He actively participated in everything, but remained totally detached, inwardly distancing himself from everything taking place around him. That is the meaning of the benign smile Krishna always had on his beautiful countenance.

During Krishna Bhava, although Amma listened to the problems of the devotees, She always had a more playful and detached attitude toward them. In that state, there was neither love nor loveless-ness, neither compassion nor compassionless-ness. The motherly affection and attachment necessary to consider the devotees' feelings and to express deep concern was not expressed. It was a state of beyond-ness. Amma thought that this wouldn't help the devotees much. Thus, She decided to love and serve Her children like a mother.

Originally, Amma manifested both Krishna and Devi Bhava, but She stopped Krishna Bhava in 1983.

"Are You Happy?"

Questioner: Amma, I have heard You ask people who come up for *darshan*, "Happy?" Why do You ask them this?

Amma: It is like an invitation to be happy. If you are happy, you are open, and then God's love, or *shakti* [divine energy], can flow into you. So, Amma is actually telling that person to be happy so God's shakti can enter him or her. When you are happy, when you are open and receptive, more and more happiness will be available to you. When you are unhappy, you are closed and you lose everything. One who is open is happy. It will draw God into you. And when God is enshrined within, you can only be happy.

A Great Example

The day we arrived in Santa Fe, it was drizzling. "It always happens in Santa Fe. After a long drought, it rains when Amma arrives," said Amma's host at the Amma Center of New Mexico.

It was dark by the time we reached the host's house. Amma was a little slow to get out of the car. As soon as Amma stepped out of the car, the host offered Amma Her sandals. He then walked toward the front of the car, hoping to lead Amma to the house.

Amma made a few steps toward the front of the car, then, suddenly, turned around, saying, "No, Amma doesn't like to walk across the front of the car. That is the face of the car. It is disrespectful to do so. Amma doesn't feel like doing that." Saying so, Amma walked around the back of the car and then to the house. This was not the only time Amma has behaved this way. Whenever Amma gets out of a car, She does this.

There is no greater example of how Amma's heart goes out to everything—even non-living objects.

Relationships

hile one person was having darshan, he turned his head toward me and said, "Please ask Amma if I can stop dating and getting into love affairs?"

Amma: (smiling mischievously) What happened, did your girlfriend run away with someone?

Questioner: (looking quite surprised) How did You know that?

Amma: Simple—that is one of the occasions in life when one will have such thoughts.

Questioner: Amma, I am jealous of my girlfriend's continued friendship with her previous boyfriend.

Amma: Is that the reason why you want to stop dating and getting into relationships?

Questioner: I am fed up and frustrated with similar occurrences in life. Enough is enough. Now I want to have peace and to focus on my spiritual practices.

Amma didn't ask anything further. She continued to give darshan. After some time, the man asked me, "I wonder if Amma has any advice for me?"

Amma heard him talking to me.

Amma: Son, Amma thought that you had already decided what to do. Didn't you say that you are fed up with such things? From now on you want to lead a peaceful life, concentrating on your spiritual practices, don't you? That sounds like the right solution. So, go ahead and do it.

The man was silent for some time, but looked restless. At one point, Amma glanced at him. Through the look and smile, I could see the Great Master in Amma whirling the legendary churning stick in Her hands, ready to stir up something and bring it to the surface.

Questioner: That means Amma has nothing to tell me, doesn't it?

Suddenly the poor fellow began to weep.

Amma: (wiping his tears) Come on, my son, what is your real problem? Open up and tell Amma.

Questioner: Amma, a year ago I met her during one of Amma's programs. When we looked into each other's eyes, we knew that we were destined to be together. That is how it started. And now, all of a sudden, this fellow—her *ex*-boyfriend—came between us. She says that he is only a friend, but there are situations when I strongly doubt her words.

Amma: What makes you feel so when she has told you otherwise?

Questioner: The situation is like this: now, both me *and* her ex-boyfriend are here to attend Amma's program. She spends more time with him than with me. I feel very upset. I don't know what to do. I am depressed. It has become difficult for me to remain focused on Amma, which is my purpose for being here. My meditations don't have the same intensity, and I am not even able to sleep well.

Amma: (joking) Do you know what? He might be praising her saying, "Look, darling, you are the most beautiful woman in the world. And I can't even think of another woman after meeting you." He might be expressing more love to her, letting her speak a lot, keeping quiet even during times when he feels provoked. On top of all, he must be buying her a lot of chocolate! Unlike with him, her impression about you could be as a bully who always picks at her and fights with her and so forth.

Hearing these words, the man and the devotees sitting around Amma had a hearty laugh. However, he was honest to confess to Amma that he was, more or less, how Amma described.

Amma: (patting his back) Do you feel a lot of anger and hatred toward her?

Questioner: Yes, I do. I feel more anger toward him. My mind gets so agitated!

Amma felt his palm. It was very hot.

Amma: Where is she now?

Questioner: Somewhere around.

Amma: (in English) Go talk.

Questioner: Now?

Amma: (in English) Yes, now.

Questioner: I don't know where she is.

Amma: (in English) Go look.

Questioner: Yes, I will. But I have to find him first, because that's where she will be. Anyway, Amma, tell me now: should I continue or end the relationship? Do you think the relationship can be restored?

Amma: Son, Amma knows that you are still attached to her. The most important thing is to convince yourself that this feeling that you call love is not love, but attachment. Only that conviction will help you come out of this agitated mental condition that you are in now. Whether you succeed or fail in restoring the relationship, if you are not able to clearly distinguish between attachment and love, you will continue to suffer.

Amma will tell you a story. A high official once visited a lunatic asylum. The doctor took him around for a tour. In one of the cells, he found a patient repeating, "Pumpum… Pumpum… Pumpum…." rocking back and forth on a chair. The officer enquired the reason for his illness and asked the doctor whether there was any connection between the name and the disease.

The doctor replied, "It is a sad story, officer. Pumpum was the girl whom he loved. She jilted him and ran away with another person. After that, he went mad."

"Poor fellow," remarked the officer and went ahead. However, he was surprised to see another patient sitting in the next cell repeating, "Pumpum... Pumpum... Pumpum..." while continuously hitting his head against the wall. Turning to the doctor, the puzzled officer asked, "What is this? How come this patient is also repeating the same name? Is there any connection?"

"Yes, sir," replied the doctor. "This is the man who finally married Pumpum."

The man burst into laughter.

Amma: Look, son, love is like the blossoming of a flower. You cannot force it to open. If you force open a flower, all the beauty and fragrance will be destroyed, and neither you nor anyone else will benefit. On the contrary, if you allow it to unfold by itself, naturally, then you can experience the sweet fragrance and the colorful petals. So, be patient, observe yourself. Be a mirror and try to see where you have gone wrong and how.

Questioner: I think my jealousy and anger will end only if I marry God.

Amma: Yes, you said it. Be God's bride. Only union with the spiritual truth will enable you to go beyond and find real peace and joy.

Questioner: Will You help me in that process?

Amma: Amma's help is always there. You only have to see it and take it.

Questioner: Thank You so much, Amma. You have already helped me.

What Does a True Master Do?

Questioner: Amma, what does a *Satguru* [True Master] do to a disciple?

Amma: A Satguru helps the disciple to see his or her weaknesses.

Questioner: How does that help the disciple?

Amma: To really see means to realize and to accept. Once the disciple accepts his or her weaknesses, it is easier to overcome them.

Questioner: Amma, when You say "weaknesses," are You referring to the ego?

Amma: Anger is a weakness; jealousy is a weakness; hatred, self-ishness and fear are all weaknesses. Yes, the root cause of all these weaknesses is ego. The mind with all its limitations and weaknesses is known as the ego.

Questioner: So, basically, You are saying that a Satguru's job is to work on the ego of the disciple.

Amma: A Satguru's job is to help the disciple realize the insignificance of this petty phenomenon known as the ego. The ego is like a flame burning from the oil in a small earthen lamp.

Questioner: Why is it important to know the insignificance of the ego?

Amma: Because there is nothing new or noteworthy about the ego. When the effulgence of the sun is available, why should one worry about this small flame that can be extinguished at any time?

Questioner: Amma, would You mind elaborating that point slightly?

Amma: You are the whole, the divinity. Compared to that, the ego is nothing but a small flame. So, on one side, a Satguru removes the ego. However, on the other side, he or she bestows the whole on you. From a beggar, the Satguru lifts you to the status of an emperor, the Emperor of the Universe. From a mere receiver, the Satguru makes you the giver, the giver of everything to those who approach you.

A Mahatma's Actions

Questioner: Is it true that whatever a Mahatma does has a meaning?

Amma: It is better to say that whatever a Self-realized soul does has a divine message, a message that conveys the deeper principles of life. Even the seemingly senseless things they do will have such a message.

There was a Mahatma whose only job was to roll big boulders up to the top of a mountain. That was the only work he did until his death. He never got bored or had any complaints. People thought he was crazy, but he wasn't. Sometimes it would take several hours or even days to single-handedly roll a boulder all the way to the top of the mountain. And once he managed to get it there, he would roll it down. Looking at the boulder rolling down from the top to the foot of the mountain, the Mahatma would clap his hands and burst into laughter like a small child.

Ascension in any field of action takes a lot of courage and energy, but it doesn't even take a moment to destroy everything that we have acquired through hard work. This is very true even about virtues. Also, this Great Soul was not at all attached to the sincere effort that he had put forth to roll this boulder uphill. This is why he could laugh like a child—the laughter of supreme detachment. Probably these are the lessons he wished to teach everyone.

People may interpret and judge a Mahatma's actions. This is only because their minds are devoid of the subtlety necessary to penetrate beneath the surface. People have expectations, but a true Mahatma cannot fulfill anyone's expectations.

Amma's Hugs Awaken

Questioner: If somebody were to say to You that they could also do the same thing that You are doing—that is hugging people—what would You answer?

Amma: That would be wonderful. The world needs more and more compassionate hearts. Amma would be happy if another person were to consider serving humanity by embracing people with true love and compassion as his or her dharma [duty]— because one Amma cannot physically embrace the entire human race. However, a true mother would never make any claims about the self-sacrifice that she makes for her children.

Questioner: Amma, what happens when You hug people?

Amma: When Amma embraces people, it is not just physical contact that is taking place. The love Amma feels for all of creation flows toward each person who comes to Her. That pure vibration of love purifies people, and this helps them in their inner awakening and spiritual growth.

Both men and women of today's world need to awaken to motherly qualities. Amma's hugs are to help people become aware of this universal need.

Love is the only language that every living being can understand. It is universal. Love, peace, meditation and *moksha* [liberation] are all universal.

How to Make the World into God

Questioner: As a family man, I have so many responsibilities and obligations. What should my attitude be?

Amma: Whether you are a family man or a monk, the most important thing is how you look at and reflect upon life and the experiences it brings. If your attitude is positive and accepting, you live with God even while in the world. Then the world becomes God, and you experience God's presence every moment. But a negative attitude will bring just the opposite result—then you choose to live with the devil. Knowing one's own mind and its lower tendencies while constantly trying to transcend them should be the focus of a sincere *sadhak* [spiritual aspirant].

A Mahatma was once asked, "Holy one, are you sure that you will go to heaven when you die?"

The Mahatma replied, "Yes, of course."

"But how do you know? You are not dead, and you don't even know what is in God's mind."

"Look here, it is true that I have no idea what is in God's mind, but I know my mind. I am always happy wherever I am. Therefore, even if I am in hell I will be happy and peaceful," replied the Mahatma.

That happiness and peace verily is heaven. Everything depends on your mind.

Power of Amma's Words

I've had this experience not once but a hundred times. Suppose somebody asks me a question or brings a serious problem to me. I try to answer the question and tackle the problem in a very descriptive and logical manner.

Expressing sincere thanks and appreciation, they walk away, seeming happy with my solution, as I watch them with a little air of self-pride. However, I soon see the same person going to another swami and asking the same question—a clear indication they were not satisfied with my advice. However, the person continues to suffer.

Eventually, they come to Amma. Amma answers the question in a similar manner. I mean, the words, sometimes even the examples, are the same. But a sudden change occurs in the person. The shadow of doubt, fear and sorrow is completed lifted, and the person's face lights up. It really makes a big difference. I always think, "What makes the difference? Amma doesn't say anything new. But the impact is tremendous."

Take, for example, the following incident: While Amma was serving lunch during a retreat, an Indian doctor who had been living in the United States for the last 25 years approached me and said, "This is my first encounter with Amma. I would like to speak to you or another swami."

The lady then proceeded to tell me a very touching story. A couple of years ago, her husband went on a pilgrimage to Mount Kailash in the Himalayas. There, he suffered a heart attack and died on the spot. The lady could not let go of the pain and sorrow. She said, "I feel angry toward God. God is ruthless." I listened to her story with as much sympathy as I could.

I spoke to her and tried to convince her of the spiritual aspects of death and shared several of Amma's examples with her.

As I concluded my counseling, I told her that, in fact, her husband was so fortunate to breathe his last at the holy abode of Lord Shiva. "He had a magnificent death," I reminded her.

Finally, when she left, the lady said, "Thank you so much. However, I still feel a lot of pain."

The next morning, the lady came for *darshan*. Before I could relate any of her story to Amma, Amma looked deep into her eyes and asked in English, "Sad?"

Amma obviously felt her deep sadness. While I told her story to Amma, Amma held the lady close to Her with so much warmth. After a few moments, Amma gently lifted the lady's face and again gazed deep into her eyes. "Death is not the end; it is not complete annihilation. It is beginning of a new life," She said. "Your husband was lucky. Amma sees him happy and peaceful. Therefore don't grieve."

The lady suddenly stopped crying and there was so much peace on her face.

That night, I saw her again. She looked so relieved. The lady said, "I am so peaceful now. Amma has really blessed me. I don't know how She could take all my sadness so suddenly,"

Later, with this in mind, I asked the following question to Amma: "Amma, how come Your words create such a big transformation? Why is it not the same when we speak?"

"Because you are married to the world and divorced from the divine."

"Amma, the mind looks for more explanations. So, will You be kind enough to elaborate a little more?"

"Married to the world means, 'identified with the mind,' which results in attachment to the diverse world and its objects. This keeps you separate, or divorced, from your inner divine nature.

"It is like a state of hypnosis. When we de-hypnotize ourselves from the mind, an inner divorce happens. In that state, you may still function in the world, but your inner marriage, or union with the divine, helps you see the false, changing nature of the world. Therefore, you remain untouched or detached. You are no longer hypnotized by the world and its objects. This indeed is the supreme state of Self-realization. It is to realize that this union, or marriage with the world, has no truth to it. Truth lies in reuniting with the divine and in remaining eternally married to it. The *gopis* [wives of the cowherds] of Vrindavan considered themselves to be brides of Lord Krishna. Internally they were married to him, the divine, and remained divorced from the world."

Scientists & Saints

o a devotee who asked a question about non-believers:

Amma: Don't we believe the scientists when they talk about the moon and Mars? Yet how many of us can really confirm what they say is true? Still, we trust the words of the scientists and the astronomers, don't we? Likewise, the saints and seers of the past performed years of experiments in their inner laboratories and realized the supreme truth, which is the substratum of the universe. Just as we trust the words of scientists who talk about facts unknown to us, so should we have faith in the words of the Great Masters who speak about the Truth, in which they are established.

How to Go Beyond Thoughts?

Questioner: Amma, it seems that there is no end to these thoughts. The more we meditate, the more thoughts come. Why is it so? How do we eliminate these thoughts and go beyond them?

Amma: Thoughts, which constitute the mind, in reality, are inert. They derive their power from the Atman. Our thoughts are our own creation. We make them real by cooperating with them. If we withdraw our support, they will dissolve. Observe the thoughts closely, without labeling them. Then you will see them gradually going away.

The mind has been accumulating thoughts and desires for ages—through the different bodies in which you have taken birth. All these emotions are buried deep within. What you see or experience on the surface of the mind is only a small portion of the hidden layers dormant within. When you try to make the mind still through meditation, these thoughts will slowly come to the surface. It is like trying to clean a floor that has been lying unwashed for a long time. Now, when we begin the process, the more we wash, the more dirt comes to the surface because the floor has been collecting dirt for years.

Likewise the mind—previously, we never paid any attention to the various thoughts that streamed through our mind. Like the dirty floor, the mind has been gathering thoughts, desires and emotions for a very long time. We are only aware of the superficial ones. However, beneath the surface, there are countless layers of thoughts and emotions. Just as more dirt comes to the surface in the process of cleaning the floor, the more thoughts become evident as our meditation gets deeper. Keep cleaning and they will disappear.

In fact, it is good if they show up. Because once you see them and recognize them, it is easier to remove them. Don't lose patience. Be persistent and keep performing your *sadhana* [spiritual practices]. In due course, you will gain the strength to surpass them.

Violence, War & The Solution

Questioner: What can people do to put an end to war and suffering?

Amma: Be more compassionate and have more understanding.

Questioner: That may not be an immediate solution.

Amma: An immediate and quick-responding solution is almost impossible. Implementation of a time-bound program also may not work.

Questioner: But that is not what the peace-loving people of the world want. They want a quick-responding solution.

Amma: That is good. Let that desire to find a quick-responding solution keep growing till it becomes an intense longing. Only from that profound longing will a quick-responding solution evolve.

Questioner: Many spiritually oriented people are of the opinion that violence or war outside is only a manifestation of the violence inside. What do You think about that?

Amma: It is true. However, one thing to be understood is that just as violence is part of the human mind, peace and happiness are also very much part of it. And if people really want, they can find peace both within and without. Why are people more focused on the aggressive and destructive aspect of the mind? Why do they completely overlook the infinite compassion and creative heights that the same mind can attain?

Ultimately speaking, all wars are nothing but the mind's craving to express its inner violence. The mind has a primitive, undeveloped or under-evolved aspect. War is the outcome of that primitive part of the mind. The warmongering nature of the mind is simply an example, proving we haven't outgrown our primitive mind yet. Unless this part is transcended, war and conflict will continue in society. Seeking the right way to outgrow this aspect of the mind and implementing it is the suitable and healthy way to approach the issue of war and violence.

Questioner: Is that way spirituality?

Amma: Yes, the way is spirituality—transforming our thinking process and outgrowing our mental weaknesses and limitations.

Questioner: Do You think people of all faiths will accept this?

Amma: Whether they accept it or not, it is the truth. Only when religious leaders take initiative to propagate the spiritual principles of their religions, will the present situation change.

Questioner: Amma, do You think that the basic principle of all religions is spirituality?

Amma: It is not Amma's thinking. It is Amma's firm belief. It is the truth.

Religion and its essential principles have not been properly understood. In fact, they have even been misinterpreted. There are two aspects for every single religion in the world: the outer and the inner. The outer is the philosophy or the intellectual part, and the inner is the spiritual part. Those who become too attached to the outside of religion will be misled. Religions are pointers. They point to a goal, and the goal is spiritual realization. In order to attain that goal, one has to transcend the pointer, that is the words.

For example, you have to cross a river. You must use a ferryboat. However, once you reach the other shore, you must get out and move forward. On the other hand, if you adamantly say, "I love this boat so much. I don't want to get out. I will remain here," then you won't reach the other shore. Religion is the boat. Use it to cross the ocean of misunderstanding and misconceptions about life. Without understanding and practicing this, true peace will not dawn, either on the outside or the inside.

Religion is like a fence that protects a sapling from animals. Once it becomes a tree, it outgrows the need for the fence. So we can say that religion is like the fence, and realization is like the tree.

Somebody points a finger toward a fruit on a tree. You look at the tip of the finger and then beyond. Unless you look beyond the fingertip, you will not obtain the fruit. In the modern-day world, people of all religions are missing the fruit. They have become too attached to, and even obsessed with, the fingertips—the words and outside aspects of their religions.

Questioner: Do You think there is not enough awareness about this in society?

Amma: There is a lot of work going on to create this awareness. But the intensity of darkness is such that we need to awaken and work harder. Of course there are individuals and organizations involved in creating this awareness. But the goal will not be achieved only by organizing conferences and peace talks. Real awareness comes only through a meditative life. It is something that should happen within. All organizations and individuals actively involved in establishing a peaceful world without war should emphasize this point. Peace is not a product of intellectual exercise. It is a feeling, rather, a blossoming that occurs within as a result of directing our energy through the proper channels. That is what meditation does.

Questioner: How would You describe the present state of affairs in the world?

Amma: In the mother's womb, the human fetus is shaped like a fish in the beginning. Then at the end it almost looks like a monkey. Although we claim to be civilized people who have taken big leaps in the scientific field, many of our actions indicate that inside we are still only at that last stage in the womb.

Actually, Amma would say that the human mind is far more advanced than that of a monkey. A monkey can jump only from one branch to another, from one tree to another, but the human monkey mind can take much bigger leaps. It can jump from here to anywhere, to the moon or to the Himalayan peaks, and from the present to the past and to the future.

Only an inner change based on a spiritual outlook will bring peace and put an end to suffering. Most people are adamant in their attitudes. Their slogan is "Only if you change, will I change." This won't help anyone. If you change first, the other person will automatically change as well.

Christ & Christianity

Questioner: I am a Christian by birth. I love Christ, but I love Amma too. You are my Guru. However, my dilemma is that my two sons, who are ardent followers of the church and Jesus, do not believe in anything other than that. They keep telling me, "Mom, we are sad because we won't see you in heaven, as you will go to hell by not following Christ." I try to talk to them, but they won't listen. Amma, what should I do?

Amma: Amma perfectly understands their faith in Christ. In fact, Amma sincerely appreciates and has a great respect for people who have deep faith in their religion and personal God. However, it is completely wrong and illogical to say that all others who don't believe in Christ will go to hell. When Christ said, "Love your neighbor as you love yourself," he didn't mean, "Love only Christians," did he? To say, "All others, except Christians will go to hell," is not considering others due to a total lack of love. This is a lie. Lying is against God. Godhood, or Godliness, is in being truthful, because God is Truth. God is in considering and loving others.

A statement such as "All of you will go to hell because you don't follow Christ" shows total disrespect and a lack of kindness to the rest of humanity. How haughty and cruel an attitude it is to say that all the great saints, sages and the billions of people who lived before Christ went to hell? Are these people claiming that experiencing God is only 2000 years old, or do they mean that even God is only 2000 years old? That is against the very nature of God, who is all-pervasive and beyond space and time.

Jesus was God manifest in human form. Amma has absolutely no problem accepting that. However, this doesn't mean that all the great incarnations before and after him are not Avatars [God descended in human form] or are incapable of saving those who have faith in them.

Didn't Christ say, "The kingdom of heaven is within"? This is such a simple and straightforward statement. What does it mean? It means God dwells within you. If heaven is within, hell is also within. It is your mind. The mind is a very effective tool. We can use it to create both hell and heaven.

All Mahatmas, including Christ, give great importance to love and compassion. In reality, love and compassion are the fundamental principles of all genuine religions. These divine qualities serve as the substratum of all faiths. Without accepting pure consciousness as the essential principle underlying everything, one cannot love and be compassionate to others. To say, "I love you, but only if you are a Christian," is like saying, "Only Christians have consciousnesses; all others are inert objects." To deny consciousness is to deny love and Truth.

Daughter, as far as your attitude towards the situation is concerned, Amma doesn't think that it will be easy to change the way your children feel. And neither is it necessary. Let them be with their faith. Follow your heart and silently continue to do what you think is right. After all, the deep feeling in your heart is what really matters.

Be a good Christian, Hindu, Buddhist, Jew or Muslim, but don't ever lose your discrimination and become a mad person in the name of religion.

Initiation into a Christ Mantra

young Christian man asked Amma for a mantra. "Who is your beloved deity?" Amma asked him.

"It is up to You, Amma. Whichever god You choose, I will chant that mantra," he said.

Amma replied, "No, Amma knows that you were born and brought up as a Christian, so that *samskara* [predominate tendency inherited from this and past lives] is deep rooted in you."

After a moment's thought, the young man said, "Amma, if You want me to choose the deity, then please initiate me into a Kali mantra."

Amma lovingly denied his request and said, "Look, Amma knows that you are trying to please Her. For Amma, it doesn't matter whether you chant a Kali mantra or Christ mantra. Be honest with yourself and be open to Amma. It is that attitude that really makes Amma happy."

"But Amma, I chant the *Mrityunjaya* mantra and other Hindu prayers," he said, trying to convince Amma.

Amma responded, "That may be true, however, you must chant a Christ mantra, as that is your predominant samskara. If you chant other mantras, you will have difficulty sticking to them in the long run. Conflicting thoughts are bound to arise."

However, the young man was adamant. He wanted Amma to either choose a mantra for him or to initiate him into a Kali mantra. Eventually, Amma said, "Okay, son, you do one thing— sit quietly and meditate for some time. Let us see what happens."

A few minutes later, after he came out of his meditation, Amma asked him, "Now, tell Amma, who is your beloved deity?" The young man only smiled. Amma asked him, "Christ, isn't it?" The boy replied, "Yes, Amma. You are right, and I am wrong."

Amma told him, "Amma sees no difference between Christ, Krishna and Kali. However, though not in your conscious mind, subconsciously you feel a difference. Amma wanted you to realize that and to accept it. That is why She asked you meditate."

The young man was happy, and Amma initiated him into a Christ mantra.

Deluded Seekers & The Way Out

Questioner: Amma, there are people who have been performing intense spiritual practices for a long time. However, they are also very deluded. Some of them even claim to have completed the journey. How can we help such people?

Amma: How can anyone help them unless they realize the need for it? In order to come out of the darkness of delusion, one should first know that he or she is in darkness. It is another complex mental state. These children are stuck there and find it difficult to accept the truth. How could one make any claims, as these children do, if he or she was totally free from all forms of ego?

Questioner: What pushes them into this deluded mental state?

Amma: Their wrong concept about spirituality and Self-enquiry.

Questioner: Can they be saved?

Amma: Only if they want to be saved.

Questioner: Can't God's grace save them?

Amma: Of course, but are they open to receive that grace?

Questioner: Grace and compassion are unconditional. To be open is a condition, isn't it?

Amma: Openness is not a condition. It is a need, as indispensable as eating and sleeping.

A True Master's Help to Complete the Journey

Questioner: Some are of the view that the guidance of a Guru is not necessary to attain God-realization. Amma, what do You think about this?

Amma: A physically blind person sees darkness everywhere. So, he seeks help. But even though people are spiritually blind, they don't understand it. Even if they understand it, they don't accept it. Therefore, it is difficult for them to seek guidance.

People have different opinions and they have the freedom to express them. Those with sharper intellects can prove or disprove many things. However, their statements may not necessarily be the truth. The more intellectual you are, the more egoistic you are. For such a person, surrendering is not so easy. The experience of God will not become a reality unless the ego is surrendered. People who are very much attached to their ego will find many ways to justify their egoistic actions. If somebody claims that a Guru's guidance is not necessary in the path to God, such a person, Amma feels, is afraid to surrender his or her ego. Or maybe they themselves crave to be a Guru.

Though our true nature is divine, we have been identified with the world of names and forms for so long, thinking them to be real. We now need to give up our identification with them.

An Innocent Heart's Offering

A little girl who came for *darshan* offered a beautiful flower to Amma. She said, "Amma, this is from our garden at home."

Amma replied, "Is that so? It is lovely." Accepting the flower from the girl, Amma humbly touched it to Her head as if bowing to it.

"Did you pluck it yourself?" Amma asked. The girl nodded.

The girl's mother explained that her daughter was so excited when she told her they were going to see Amma that she rushed to the garden and returned with the flower. Indeed, the flower still had a few dewdrops on it. "Showing me the flower, she said, 'Mom, this flower is as beautiful as Amma.'"

The girl was sitting on Amma's lap. She suddenly embraced Amma tightly and kissed Her on both cheeks. She said, "I love You so much, Amma." Returning several kisses back, Amma replied, "My child, Amma loves you a lot too."

Watching the little girl gleefully dancing next to her mother as they walked back to their seats, Amma said, "Innocence is so beautiful and heart-capturing."

Hotline to God

uring the question-and-answer session on one of Amma's retreats, one of the devotees said in a concerned tone, "Amma, so many thousands of people pray to You. It seems that almost all the lines will be busy when I call for help. Do You have any suggestions for me?"

Hearing the question, Amma laughed heartily and replied, "Don't worry, son. You have a direct line." Amma's answer evoked an uproarious laughter. She continued, "In fact, everyone has a hotline to God. However, the quality of the line depends on the fervor of your prayer."

Like a River Flowing...

Questioner: Amma, You keep doing the same job day after day, year after year. Don't You get bored continuously hugging people like this?

Amma: If the river feels bored of flowing, if the sun feels bored of illumining, and if the wind feels bored of blowing, then Amma, too, feels bored.

Questioner: Amma, wherever You are, You are always surrounded by people. Don't you feel the need for a little freedom and aloneness?

Amma: Amma is always free and alone.

Vedic Sounds & Mantras

uestioner: The ancient *Rishis* [Sages] are known as *mantra drishtas* [those who have seen the mantras]. Does this mean that they have seen the pure sounds and mantras?

Amma: "Seen" means "dawned within" or experienced. Mantras can only be experienced internally. The Vedic sounds and mantras were already there in the universe, in the atmosphere. What do scientists do when they invent something? They bring a fact that has been lying hidden for so long to light. We cannot call it a new invention. They only uncover it.

The only differences scientific inventions and mantras are the subtler levels. The Rishis, through severe penance, made their inner instruments clear and completely pure. Thus, these universal sounds automatically dawned within them.

We know how sounds and images in the form of vibrations travel through the air from a radio station or TV station. They always remain in the atmosphere. However, to view and hear them, we need to tune our instrument, the radio or TV. Likewise, these divine sounds will reveal themselves to those who have a clear and pure mind. The external eyes are powerless to see them. Only by developing a third eye, or inner eye, will we be able to experience these sounds.

Let it be any sound, learn to feel it as deep as you can. Feeling the sound, not merely hearing the sound, is what really matters. Feel your prayers, feel your mantra and you will feel God.

Questioner: Do mantras have a meaning?

Amma: Not in the way you think or expect. Mantras are the purest form of universal vibrations, or *shakti* [divine energy], the profundity of which was experienced by the Rishis in deep meditation. Mantra is the power of the universe in seed form. That is why they are known as *bijaksharas* [seed letters]. Having gone through that experience, they offered these pure sounds to humanity. However, verbally encapsulating an experience, particularly the most profound of all experiences, is not so easy. So, the mantras we have are the closest sounds to the universal sound that the compassionate Rishis could verbally create for the benefit of the world. However, the fact still remains that the fullness of a mantra can only be experienced when your mind attains perfect purity.

Something Lacking

Questioner: Amma, so many people say that in spite of all their material comforts, there's something lacking in their lives. Why do they feel this way?

Amma: Life brings various experiences and situations to different people according to their past karma [actions] and the way they live and act in the present. Whoever you are or whatever material heights you gain, only living and thinking in a dharmic [righteous] way will help you attain perfection and happiness in life. If your wealth and desires are not used in accordance with the ultimate dharma, that is the obtaining of *moksha* [liberation], you will never have peace. You will always have the feeling "I lack something." That something you lack is peace, fulfillment and contentment. And this lack of true joy creates a void that cannot possibly be filled by indulging in pleasures or fulfilling material desires.

People all over the world think that they can fill this gap by fulfilling their desires. In fact, that gap will remain and might even broaden if they keep running after worldly objects alone.

Dharma and moksha are interdependent. One who lives according to the principles of dharma will attain moksha, and one who has a desire to attain moksha will invariably lead a dharmic life.

If they are used incorrectly and unwisely, money and riches can become big obstacles. They are obstructions to those who wish to evolve spiritually. The more money you have, the more obsessed you are likely to become with your body. The more you identify with the body, the more egoistic you become. Money is not a problem, but unintelligent attachment to it is.

World and God

Questioner: What is the connection between the world and God, happiness and sorrow?

Amma: In fact, the world is needed to know God or to experience real happiness. In a classroom, the teacher writes on a blackboard with a white piece of chalk. The black background provides the contrast for the white letters. Similarly, the world is the background for us to know our purity, to become aware of our true nature, which is eternal happiness.

Questioner: Amma, is it true that only human beings feel unhappy or discontent; animals don't?

Amma: Not really. Animals too have feelings of sorrow and discontentment. They experience sorrow, love, anger and other emotions. However, they don't feel them as deeply as human beings. Humans are more evolved, so they feel it in a much more profound way.

Actually, deep feelings of sorrow show the potential to move to the other extreme of bliss. From that feeling of deep sorrow and pain, we can, in fact, gather enough strength to move to the path of Self-enquiry. It is just a question of channeling our *shakti* [vital force] with more discrimination.

Questioner: Amma, how can we use our shakti with more discrimination?

Amma: Only deeper understanding will help us do that. Suppose we participate in a funeral ceremony or visit a sick, elderly person who is completely bedridden. We will definitely feel sad. However, by the time we are back home and engaged in our duties, we will have forgotten them and moved on. The scene hasn't touched the innermost recesses of our heart; it hasn't gone deep. However, if you can really contemplate on such experiences, thinking, "The same thing will happen to me sooner or later. I should enquire into the cause of all these sorrows and prepare myself before it is too late," then they will gradually change your life and direct you to the deeper mysteries of the universe. Gradually, if you are serious and sincere, you will find the very source of joy.

As Amma was talking, a child who was comfortably sitting in its mother's lap suddenly started crying. Calling out, "Baby...baby...baby," Amma asked why the child was crying. Lifting the pacifier in her hands, the mother said, "She lost this." Everyone laughed. Then the mother put the pacifier back in the child's mouth and it stopped crying.

Amma: The little one lost her happiness. That was a good demonstration of the point we were trying to clarify. The pacifier is illusory, like the world. It doesn't give any nourishment to the child. However, it stops the child from crying. So, we can say that it has a purpose, so to speak. Likewise, the world doesn't really nourish the soul. But it has a purpose, which is to remind us of the Creator, or God.

Questioner: It is said that one is bound to go through immense pain and sorrow before the realization of Self. Is this statement correct?

Amma: Even otherwise there is sorrow and pain in life. Spirituality is not a journey forward; it is a journey backward. We return to our original source of existence. In that process, we have to pass through the layers of emotions and *vasanas* [tendencies] we have accumulated so far. That is where the pain comes from, not from outside. By going through those layers with an open attitude, we are, in fact, crossing over and transcending them, which will ultimately take us to the abode of supreme peace and bliss.

Before reaching the top of a mountain, one has to be in the valley at the foot of the mountain, the other extreme. Likewise, before attaining the peak of happiness, the experience of the other end, that is sorrow, is unavoidable.

Questioner: Why is it unavoidable?

Amma: As long as identification with ego exists and as long as one feels, "I am separate from God," there will be pain and sorrow. Now you are standing at the foot of the mountain. Before you can even start climbing the mountain, you need to relinquish your attachments with the valley and whatever you own there. Pain is unavoidable only when you do it half-heartedly.

Otherwise, there is no pain. When that attachment is renounced, the pain becomes an intense longing, the longing to reach the heights of eternal union. The real question is, how many can give up that attachment whole-heartedly?

The devotee spent a few thoughtful moments. Noticing his silence, Amma tapped on his head, saying, "Tuning the drum of the ego, let pleasing sounds come from it." The devotee spontaneously burst into laughter.

Amma: Amma has heard a story. There was a rich man who lost all interest in worldly life and wanted to start a new life of peace and tranquility. He had everything that money could buy, but still life proved utterly meaningless to him. So he decided to take the guidance of a Spiritual Master. Before leaving his house, the man thought, "What am I going to do with all this money? Let me offer everything to the Master and forget about it. What I really crave is true happiness." So the rich man put all the gold coins he had in a bag and carried it along with him.

After a whole day's journey, the man found the Master sitting under a tree in the outskirts of a village. He placed the moneybag in front of the Master and bowed down to him. But when he raised his head, the man was astounded to see the Master running away with the moneybag. Totally confused and startled by the Guru's strange behavior, the rich man chased him as fast as his legs could carry him. The Master ran faster—along the fields, up and down the hills, jumping over the creeks, trampling the bushes and through the streets. It was getting dark. The Master was so familiar with the village's narrow, winding system of paths and lanes that the rich man had great difficulty keeping up with him.

Finally, giving up all hope, the rich man returned to the same spot where he first met the Master. And there lay his moneybag—and, hiding behind the tree, was the Master. As the rich man greedily grabbed his precious bag of money, the Master peeped from behind the tree and said, "Tell me how you feel now."

"I am happy, very happy—it's the happiest moment in my life."

"So,"said the Guru, "to experience real happiness, one must go through the other extreme also."

Children, you can wander in the world, running after its various objects. However, unless you return to the source from where you originally started, real happiness won't happen. This is yet another moral of this story.

Questioner: Amma, I have heard that unless all seeking stops, true happiness cannot be found. How do you explain this?

Amma: "All seeking should stop" means seeking happiness in the outside world should stop, because what you are seeking is within you. Stop running after the objects of the world and turn inward. There you will find what you are seeking.

You are both the seeker and the sought. You are searching for something that you already have. It cannot be found outside. Therefore, every search for happiness outside will result in failure and frustration. It is like the dog chasing its own tail.

Unlimited Patience

here is a man in his late fifties who has been a regular visitor to Amma's programs in New York since 1988. I cannot forget him because he always has the same questions for Amma. And almost every time I wind up being his interpreter. Year after year, the man has been asking the following three questions, without even rephrasing them once:

1. Can Amma give me instant Self-realization?

2. When will I get married to a pretty woman?

3. How can I make quick money and become rich?

Seeing him coming up in the darshan line, I jokingly commented, "The broken record is coming."

Amma immediately sensed to whom I was referring. She sternly looked at me and said, "Spirituality is all about feeling and participating in the problems and pains of others. One should at least have a mature intellectual approach toward people who go through such problems and situations. If you don't have the patience to listen to them, you are not fit to be Amma's translator."

I sincerely sought Amma's forgiveness for my prejudiced attitude and words. However, I was still doubtful if Amma wanted to hear his question for the 15th time.

"Should I take his questions?" I asked Amma.

"Of course, why ask?"

For sure, they were the same three questions. And I was once again filled with awe and wonder as I witnessed Amma listening to him and giving him advice as if She was hearing his questions for the first time.

Questioner: Can Amma give me instant Self-realization?

Amma: Have you been meditating regularly?

Questioner: Hoping to make some good money, I work 50 hours a week. However, I meditate, but not regularly.

Amma: That means?

Questioner: After attending to my daily work, if I find time, I meditate.

Amma: Okay, what about repeating your mantra? Do you chant it daily as instructed?

Questioner: (with some hesitation) Yes, I chant my mantra, but not everyday.

Amma: What time do you go to bed and when do you get up in the morning?

Questioner: I usually go to bed around midnight and get up at 7: 00.

Amma: What time do you leave for work?

Questioner: My office hours are 8:30 to 5:00. It is a 35- to 40-minute drive without traffic. So I normally leave the house around 7:35 a.m. After I get up there is just enough time to make a cup of coffee, toast two pieces of bread and get dressed. With my breakfast and cup of coffee in hand, I jump into the car and drive off.

Amma: What time do you come home from work?

Question: *Mmm...* 5:30 or 6:00.

Amma: What do you do after coming home?

Questioner: I relax for half an hour and cook dinner.

Amma: For how many people?

Questioner: Just for me. I am alone.

Amma: How long does it take?

Questioner: Roughly, 40 minutes to one hour.

Amma: That is 7:30. What will you do after dinner? Watch TV?

Questioner: That is right.

Amma: For how long?

Questioner: (laughing) Amma, You cornered me. I watch TV until I go to bed. I also want to confess another thing to You.... No, forget it.

Amma: (patting him on his back) Come on, go ahead and finish what you were going to say.

Questioner: It is too embarrassing to disclose.

Amma: Okay, fine.

Questioner: (after a few moments pause) There is no point in hiding it from You. Anyways, I believe that You already know this. Otherwise, why did You even create such a situation? Oh my, it is such a *leela* [divine play].... Amma, I seek Your forgiveness, but I forgot my Guru mantra. I cannot even find the piece of paper it was written on.

Hearing his words, Amma burst into laughter.

Questioner: (puzzled) What? Why are you laughing?

As he sat with a worried look on his face, Amma jokingly pinched his ear.

Amma: You little thief! Amma knew you were trying to hide something from Her. Look, my son, God is the giver of everything. Amma understands your sincerity and inquisitiveness, but you must have more *shraddha* [loving faith and attention] and commitment, and you must be willing to work hard in order to attain the Goal, to attain Self-realization.

Mantra is the bridge that connects you to your Guru—the finite to the infinite. Repetition of Guru mantra is like food for a true disciple. Show your respect to the mantra and your worshipful attitude toward your Guru by unfailingly chanting the mantra everyday. Unless you are committed, Self-realization will not happen. Spirituality should not be a part-time job. It must be a full-time job. Amma is not asking you to resign your job or to work less. You consider your job and making money a serious affair, don't you? In a similar manner, God realization is also serious. Just like eating and sleeping, spiritual practices should become part and parcel of your life.

Questioner: (politely) Amma, I accept Your answer. I will remember that and try to put things straight as you instructed. Please bless me.

The man was quiet for sometime. He seemed to be contemplating.

Amma: Son.... You have married twice before, haven't you?

Questioner: (taken aback) How did You know?

Amma: Son, this is not the first time you've mentioned these problems to Amma.

Questioner: What a memory!

Amma: What makes you think that the next marriage will work?

Questioner: I don't know.

Amma: You don't know? Or are you uncertain?

Questioner: I am uncertain.

Amma: Even in the face of this uncertainty are you still thinking of another marriage?

Greatly puzzled and, at the same time, amused, the man almost fell down laughing. He then sat up and, with palms joined, said, "Amma, You are irresistible and undefeatable. I bow down to You."
Benignly smiling, Amma playfully tapped the man on his bald head, which he had hung down low.

Unconditional Love & Compassion

Questioner: Amma, what is Your definition of unconditional love and compassion?

Amma: It is a totally undefinable state.

Questioner: Then, what is it?

Amma: It is expansiveness, like the sky.

Questioner: Is it the inner sky?

Amma: There is no inside and outside there.

Questioner: Then?

Amma: There is only oneness. That is why it cannot be defined.

The Easiest Path

Questioner: Amma, there are so many paths, which is the easiest?

Amma: The easiest path is being by the side of a *Satguru* [True Master]. Being with a Satguru is like traveling in a Concorde Jet. A Satguru is the fastest vehicle for taking you to the Goal. Following any path without the help of a Satguru is like traveling in a shuttle-service bus, which will have a hundred stops. This will delay the process.

Enlightenment, Surrender & Living in the Present

Questioner: Is it impossible for enlightenment to occur without the attitude of surrender, no matter how intense one's *sadhana* [spiritual practices] may be?

Amma: Tell Amma, what do you mean by intense sadhana? To do intense sadhana means to perform it with sincerity and love. For this, you need to be in the present. To be in the present, you have to surrender the past and future.

Whether you call it surrender, present moment, here and now, moment-to-moment living or another term, they all are one and the same. The terms may differ, but what happens inside is the same. Any form of spiritual practice we do is to help us learn the great lesson of letting go. True meditation is not an action; it is an intense longing of the heart to be one with the Self, or God. In that process, the deeper we go, the less ego we have and the lighter we feel. So, you see, the very purpose of sadhana is to gradually remove the feeling of "I" and "mine." This process is described in different ways, using different terms, that's all.

Questioner: All material achievements and success in the world basically depend on how aggressive you are and how competent you are. Unless you keep sharpening your mind and intellect, you cannot win. A little dullness will push you to the back row, and you will be sidelined. It seems that there is a big difference between the principles of spiritual life and those of worldly life.

Amma: Daughter, as you rightly said, it only *seems* different.

Questioner: How?

Amma: Because, irrespective of who they are or what they are doing, most people do live in the present, just not fully. When they are engaged in an action or thought, they are surrendered to that moment. Otherwise, things won't happen. Look at a carpenter, for example. While using a tool, if the carpenter's mind is not focused in the present, some serious injury may occur. So, people are living in the present. The only difference is most people have little or no awareness, and therefore they are only partially present or not at all present. Spiritual science teaches us to be fully in the present moment, irrespective of time and place. People are either in the mind or in the intellect—never in the heart.

Questioner: But to be fully present doesn't one have to transcend the ego?

Amma: Yes, but transcending the ego doesn't mean you become functionless or useless. On the contrary, you will go beyond all weaknesses. You will completely be transformed and your inner capacities will express themselves to the fullest. As a perfect human being, you will be ready to serve the world, seeing no differences whatsoever.

Questioner: So, Amma, what You are saying is that basically there is no difference between surrender and living in the present?

Amma: Yes, they are one and the same.

Japa Mala & Cell Phone

Walking toward the program hall accompanied by Her children, Amma noticed one of the brahmacharis stepping aside to attend to a phone call that he had just received.

When the brahmachari finished his conversation and rejoined the group, Amma remarked, "With various responsibilities to discharge, like organizing Amma's programs across the country and contacting local coordinators, it is okay if a spiritual seeker has a cell phone. However, while holding a cell phone in one hand, keep a *japa mala* [rosary] in the other, which will remind you not to forget to chant your mantra. A cell phone is required to be in touch with the world. Use one, if necessary. But never lose contact with God. That is your life-force.

A Living Upanishad

Questioner: How do You describe a *Satguru* [True Master]?

Amma: A Satguru is a living *Upanishad* [an embodiment of the supreme truth, as depicted in the *Upanishads*].

Questioner: What is the Master's main job?

Amma: His or her sole purpose is to inspire the disciples and to instill the faith and love necessary for them to reach the Goal. Creating the fire of Self-enquiry or love for God in the disciple is the first and foremost task of the Master. Once it is kindled, the Master's next job is to keep the flame ablaze, protecting it from the stormy nights and the heavy downpour of unnecessary temptations. The Master will guard the disciple like a hen protecting the chicks under her wing. By and by, the disciple will learn greater lessons of surrender and detachment by observing the Master and drawing inspiration from his or her life. This will eventually culminate in complete surrender and transcendence.

Questioner: What does the disciple transcend?

Amma: His or her lower nature, or *vasanas* [tendencies].

Questioner: Amma, how would You describe the ego?

Amma: Just as a petty phenomenon—but a destructive one if you are not careful.

Questioner: But isn't it a very useful and powerful instrument while living in the world?

Amma: Yes, if you learn how to use it properly.

Questioner: What do you mean by "properly"?

Amma: Amma means that one should exercise proper control over it through discrimination.

Questioner: *Sadhaks* [spiritual seekers] do the same thing as part of their spiritual practice, don't they?

Amma: Yes, but a sadhak gradually gains mastery over the ego.

Questioner: Does that mean that there is no need to transcend the ego?

Amma: Gaining mastery and transcending are the same. In reality, there is nothing to transcend. Just as the ego is ultimately unreal, the transcendence is also unreal. The Atman [Self] alone is real. The rest are just shadows, or like clouds covering the sun. They are not real.

Questioner: But shadows give us shade. We cannot call them unreal, can we?

Amma: True. A shadow cannot be called unreal. It has a purpose. It gives shade. But don't forget the tree, which is the source of the shadow. The shadow cannot exist without the tree, but the tree is, even without the shadow. Therefore the shadow is neither real nor unreal. That is what *maya* [illusion] is. The mind, or ego, is neither real nor unreal. Nevertheless, the existence of the Atman doesn't depend in any way upon the ego.

For example, a man and his son are walking in a hot spell. In order to protect himself from the heat, the little boy walks behind his father, and the shadow serves him as a shade. Son, you are correct, the shadow cannot be called unreal; yet neither is it real. However, it has a purpose. In a similar way, even though the ego is neither real nor unreal, it has a function—that is to remind us of the ultimate reality, the Atman, which serves as the substratum of the ego.

Just like the shadow, neither the world nor the ego can exist without the Atman. The Atman offers the support and sustains the entire existence.

Questioner: Amma, going back to the subject of transcendence— You said that just as the ego is unreal, transcendence of the ego is also unreal. If so, what is this process of Self-unfolding, or Self-realization?

Amma: Just as the ego is unreal, so too the process of transcending the ego also only appears to take place. Even the term "Self-unfoldment" is wrong, as the Self doesn't need to unfold. That which always remains as it is, in all three periods of time, needn't undergo any such process.

All explanations eventually lead you to the realization that all explanations are meaningless. In the end you will realize that nothing else existed but the Atman, and there actually was no process.

For example, there is a beautiful spring of ambrosial water in the middle of a dense forest. One day you discover it, drink the water and attain immortality. The spring was always there, but you never knew it. You suddenly became conscious of it, aware of its existence. It is the same with the inner source of pure *shakti* [energy]. As your search and your longing to know your Self mounts, a revelation happens and you come into contact with that source. Once the connection is established, the realization that you were never disconnected from it also takes place.

For instance, the universe has immense wealth hidden in its bosom. There are priceless stones, magic potions, cure-all medicines, valuable information regarding the history of humanity, methods to solve the mystery of the universe and so forth. What the scientists of the past, present and future can discover is only an infinitesimal part of what the universe really carries within. Nothing is new. All inventions are nothing but a process of removing the cover. Likewise, the supreme truth remains deep within us, as though covered. The uncovering process is known as *sadhana* [spiritual practices].

So, from the individual's point of view, there is a process of Self-unfoldment and hence there is transcendence as well.

Questioner: Amma, how do You explain transcendence in the various day-to-day situations of life?

Amma: Transcendence occurs only when we attain enough maturity and understanding. These come through spiritual practices and by facing the different experiences and situations in life with a positive attitude and a certain degree of openness. This will help us drop our wrong notions and go beyond. If you become a little more watchful, you will understand that this dropping and going beyond smaller things, petty desires and attachments is a common experience in our daily life.

A child always likes to play with his toys—say, with his stuffed chimpanzee. He loves the stuffed chimp so much that he carries it around with him all day long. As he plays with it, he sometimes even forgets to eat. And if his mother tries to take the doll away from him, he gets so upset that he cries. The little boy even falls asleep tightly embracing it. Only then can his mother take the stuffed chimpanzee away from him.

But one day the mother sees all the toys, including the chimpanzee that the boy loved the most, lying abandoned in a corner of his room. The boy has suddenly outgrown them; he has transcended the toys. One may even see him smiling and looking at another child playing with the toys. He must be thinking, "Look at that child playing with the toys." He even has forgotten that he too was once a child.

In the case of a child, he or she drops the toys and embraces something more advanced, perhaps a three-wheeler. And before long, he or she has transcended that as well and is riding a bicycle. And then, finally, they may want a motorbike, a car and so on. But a sadhak needs to develop the strength and understanding to transcend everything that comes his or her way and embrace only the Supreme.

Maya

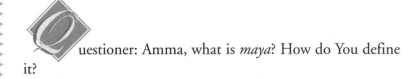

Questioner: Amma, what is *maya*? How do You define it?

Amma: The mind is maya. The inability of the mind to conceive of the world as impermanent and changing is known as maya.

Questioner: It is also said that this objective world is maya.

Amma: Yes, because it is a projection of the mind. That which prevents us from seeing this reality is maya.

A lion made of sandalwood is real to a child, but to a grownup, it's a piece of sandalwood. For the child, the wood is concealed, revealing only the lion. The parents may also enjoy the lion, but they know it is not real. For them, the wood is real, not the lion. In the same way, to a Self-realized soul, the entire universe is nothing but the essence, the "wood" that comprises everything, the Absolute Brahman, or consciousness.

Atheists

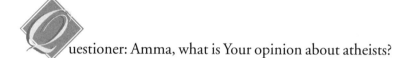

Questioner: Amma, what is Your opinion about atheists?

Amma: It doesn't matter if one believes in God or not as long as he or she properly serves society.

Questioner: You don't really care, do You?

Amma: Amma cares about everyone.

Questioner: But do You think their views are correct?

Amma: What does it matter what Amma thinks, as long as they still believe their views?

Questioner: Amma, You are slipping away without answering my question.

Amma: And, daughter, you are chasing Amma to get the answer you want.

Questioner: (laughing) Okay, Amma, I want to know if atheism is only an intellectual exercise or if there is any sense in what they say.

Amma: Sense and senselessness depend on one's attitude. Atheists strongly believe that there is no supreme power, or God. However, some of them simply say this in public, while on the inside they are believers.

There is nothing special in such intellectual exercises. An intellectually sharp person can seemingly prove or disprove the existence of God. Atheism is based on logic. How can intellectual exercises prove or disprove God, who is beyond the realm of the intellect?

Questioner: So, Amma, what You are saying is that their views about God are incorrect, aren't You?

Amma: Whether it is theirs or somebody else's, views about God are bound to be incorrect, because God cannot be viewed from a certain angle. God will appear only when all views disappear. Intellectual logic can be used to establish or refute something. But that may not always be the truth.

Suppose you say, "A has nothing in his hands. B, too, has nothing in his hands. I don't see anything in C's hands either. Therefore, nobody has anything in their hands." This is logical and sounds correct, but is it so? Similar are intellectual conclusions.

The modern-day atheists waste a lot of their time trying to prove the non-existence of God. If they are firm in their belief, why are they so worried? Instead of engaging in intellectual arguments that are destructive, they should do something beneficial to society.

Peace

Questioner: What is peace in Amma's words?

Amma: Are you asking about peace within or peace without?

Questioner: I want to know what real peace is.

Amma: Daughter, tell Amma what your version of real peace is first.

Questioner: I think peace is happiness.

Amma: But what is true happiness? Is it something that you get when your desires are fulfilled, or do you have another explanation for it?

Questioner: *Hmm...* It is a mood that comes when desires are fulfilled, isn't it?

Amma: But such happy moods will soon disappear. You feel happy when a particular desire is fulfilled. However, very soon another desire will take its place and you will find yourself running after it. There is no end to this process, is there?

Questioner: That is true. So, is feeling happy inside real happiness?

Amma: Okay, but how do you feel happy inside?

Question: (laughing) You are trying to corner me.

Amma: No, we are getting close to the answer you need. Come on, daughter, how is it possible to feel happy inside if the mind is not calm? Or do you think feeling calm and composed while eating chocolate and ice cream is real peace?

Questioner: (laughing) Oh, no, You are teasing me.

Amma: No, daughter, Amma is serious.

Questioner: (thoughtfully) That is neither peace nor happiness. That is just a sort of excitement or fascination.

Amma: Does that kind of fascination stay with you long?

Questioner: No, it comes and goes.

Amma: Now, tell Amma, can a feeling that comes and goes be called real or permanent?

Questioner: Not really.

Amma: Then what do you call it?

Questioner: That which comes and goes is usually known as "temporary" or "passing."

Amma: As you have said that, let Amma ask you this: Are there any moments in your life when you have experienced peace for no particular reason?

Questioner: (after a few thoughtful moments) Yes, once I was sitting in the backyard of my house, looking at the setting sun. It filled my heart with an unknown joy. In that beautiful moment, I simply glided into a state of thoughtlessness, and I felt so much peace and joy within. Recapturing that moment, I even wrote a poem describing the experience.

Amma: Daughter, that is the answer to your question. Peace happens when the mind is still, with fewer thoughts. Fewer thoughts mean more peace, and more thoughts mean less peace. Peace or happiness for no reason is real peace and happiness.

Peace and happiness are synonyms. The more open you are, the more peace or happiness you feel, and vice versa. Unless we have a certain degree of mastery over the mind, true peace is difficult to attain.

To find peace within is the real path to finding peace without. The inner and the outer efforts should go hand in hand.

Questioner: Amma, how do You describe peace from a spiritual point of view?

Amma: There is no difference between spiritual peace and worldly peace. Just as love is one, peace is also one. Yes, there is a difference in degree. That depends how deep you go inside. Consider the mind as a lake; the thoughts are the ripples on the lake. Each thought or movement of agitation is like a stone thrown into the lake, creating countless ripples. A meditative mind will become like a lotus flower floating on that lake. The ripples of thoughts will still be there, but the lotus is unaffected. It will just float.

"Leave me alone! I want peace!" This is a common expression we hear—sometimes in the middle of a quarrel, or when someone is fed up with another person or situation. But is it possible? Even if we leave that person alone, he won't experience any peace, nor can he really ever be alone. Behind the closed doors of his room, he will sit and brood about all that has happened, continuing to boil within. He will again be in the world of disturbing thoughts. Real peace is a profound feeling that engulfs the heart when we are free from the thoughts of the past.

Peace is not the opposite of agitation. It is the absence of agitation. It is a completely relaxed and restful state.

The Greatest Lesson in Life

Questioner: What is the greatest lesson that one needs to learn in life?

Amma: Be attached to the world with a detached attitude.

Questioner: How can attachment and detachment go together?

Amma: Attach and detach as you wish—act, then let go and move forward... act again, then let go and move forward. Extra luggage will make your journey uncomfortable, right? Likewise, the extra luggage of indiscriminate dreams, desires and attachments will make your life's journey extremely miserable.

Even great emperors, dictators and rulers suffer horribly at the end of their lives due to carrying such extra luggage in life. Nothing but the art of detachment will help you to be in a restful state of mind at that time.

Alexander was a great warrior and ruler who had conquered nearly one-third of the world. He wanted to become the emperor of the entire world, but he was defeated in battle and fell sick with a terminal illness. A few days before his death, Alexander called his ministers and explained to them how he wanted to be buried. He told them that he wanted openings made on both sides of his coffin, through which his arms should be kept hanging out with the palms turned up. The ministers asked him why he wanted this to be done. Alexander replied that, in this way, everyone would come to know that the great Alexander, who had strived his whole life to possess and conquer the world, had left it totally empty-handed. He had not even taken his own body with him. Therefore, they would understand how futile it is to spend one's whole life chasing after the world and its objects.

After all, in the end we cannot take anything with us, not even our own body. So, what is the use of feeling overly attached?

Art & Music

Questioner: Amma, being an artist, a musician, I would like to know what my attitude toward my profession should be and how to express more and more of my musical talents?

Amma: Art is God's beauty manifested in the form of music, painting, dance and so forth. It is one of the easiest ways to realize one's inherent divinity.

There are many saints who found God through music. So, you are specially blessed to be a musician. In regards to your attitude toward your profession, be a beginner, a child in front of God, in front of the divine. This will enable you to tap into the infinite possibilities of your mind. And this, in turn, will help you manifest more and more of your musical talents in a much deeper way.

Questioner: But, Amma, how to be a child, a beginner?

Amma: Just by accepting and recognizing your ignorance, you automatically become a beginner.

Questioner: I understand that, but I am not completely ignorant. I am a trained musician.

Amma: How much training do you have?

Questioner: I studied music for six years and have been a performing artist for the last 14 years.

Amma: How big is space?

Questioner: (sounding a little puzzled) I don't understand Your question.

Amma: (smiling) You don't understand the question because you don't understand space, isn't it so?

Questioner: (shrugging his shoulders) Maybe.

Amma: Maybe?

Questioner: But what is the connection between my question and Your asking, "How big is space?"

Amma: There is a connection. Pure music is as big as space. It is God. It is pure knowledge. It is the secret of allowing the pure sound of the universe to flow through you. You cannot learn music in 20 years. You may have been singing for the last 20 years, but to truly understand music means to realize music as your own Self. In order to realize music as your Self, you need to allow music to completely possess you. For more music to occupy your heart, you need to create more space within. More thoughts mean less space. Now, contemplate on this, "How much space do I have within me to spare for pure music?"

If you really wish more and more of your musical talents to manifest, lessen the quantity of unnecessary thoughts and allow more space for the energy of music to flow within you.

Wellspring of Love

Questioner: Amma, how does one learn to have pure, innocent love, as You say?

Amma: Only something that is alien to you can be learned. But love is your true nature. Within you, there is a wellspring of love. Tap that source in the right way and the *shakti* [energy] of divine love will fill your heart, expanding endlessly within you. You cannot *make* it happen; you can only create the right attitude within yourself for it to happen.

Why Do You Hug?

Questioner: Amma, You hug everyone. Who hugs You?

Amma: The entire creation hugs Amma. In reality, Amma and creation are in an eternal embrace.

Questioner: Amma, why do You hug people?

Amma: The question is like asking the river, "Why do you flow?"

Every Moment a Precious Lesson

he morning *darshan* was in progress. Amma had just finished answering Her children's questions—there had been a long line. With a deep sigh, I was about to take a break, when a devotee suddenly came forward and handed me a note. It was yet another question. To be very honest, I was a little bit annoyed. However, I took the note from him and inquired, "Can you wait until tomorrow? We are done for this morning."

He said, "It is important. Why don't you ask now?" I thought, or maybe imagined, that he was demanding.

"Do I have to explain that to you?" I retorted.

He wouldn't give up. "You are not obliged to, but why can't you ask Amma? Maybe Amma is willing to answer my question."

At this point I just ignored him and looked in the other direction. Amma was giving darshan. Our argument took place behind the darshan chair. Both of us spoke softly, but sternly.

Suddenly, Amma turned around and asked me, "Are you tired? Feeling sleepy? Did you eat?" I was stunned and, at the same time, ashamed because She had overheard the conversation. In fact, I had been foolish. I should have known better. Even though Amma was giving darshan and we were speaking softly, Her eyes, ears and Her whole body sees, hears and feels everything.

Amma continued, "If you are tired, go take a break, but take that son's question first. Learn to be considerate. Don't be obsessed with what you feel is right."

I apologized to the man and took his question. Amma lovingly addressed his problem and the man left contented. Of course, the question was an important one, as he had said.

After he left, Amma said, "Look, my son, when you react to someone, you are wrong and, most likely, they are right. He or she, who is in a better state of mind, has the clarity to observe the situation. Reaction makes you blind. Your reactive attitude doesn't help you see others or to consider their feelings.

"Before reacting to a particular situation, can you pause and tell the other person, 'Give me some time before I answer you. Let me contemplate on what you said. Maybe you are right and I am wrong'? If you have the courage to say this, you are at least considering the other person's feelings. This will prevent many unpleasant events that could arise later."

I witnessed yet another priceless lesson from the Great Master. I was humbled.

Understanding an Enlightened Being

Questioner: Is it possible to understand a Mahatma with our mind?

Amma: First of all, a Mahatma cannot be understood. He or she can only be experienced. With its vacillating and doubting nature, the mind cannot experience anything as it is, even if it is a worldly object. For example, when you want to truly experience a flower, the mind stops and something beyond the mind starts functioning.

Questioner: Amma, You said, "the mind stops and something beyond the mind starts functioning." What is that?

Amma: Call it the heart, but it is a state of temporary deep silence—a stillness of the mind, a stop in the flow of thoughts.

Questioner: Amma when You say "mind," what do You mean? Does it mean only the thoughts or does it signify more?

Amma: Mind includes memory, that is the storehouse of the past, thinking, doubting, determining and the feeling of "I."

Questioner: What about all the emotions?

Amma: They, too, are part of the mind.

Questioner: Okay, so when You say "the mind cannot understand a Mahatma," You mean this complex mechanism cannot know the state where a Mahatma is established.

Amma: Yes. The human mind is so unpredictable and tricky. It is most important for a seeker of Truth to know that he or she cannot recognize a *Satguru* [True Master]. There are no criteria to do that. A drunk can recognize another drunk. Likewise two gamblers will understand each other. One miser can recognize another miser. They all are of the same mental caliber. But no such criteria are available to recognize a Satguru. Neither our external eyes nor our mind can behold a great being. Special training is needed for that. That is *sadhana* [spiritual practice]. Only constant sadhana will help us gain the power to penetrate and go beneath the surface of the mind. Once you go beneath the surface of the mind, you will be confronted with countless layers of emotions and thoughts. To pass through and go beyond all these intricate, gross and subtle levels of the mind, the *sadhak* [spiritual aspirant] needs the continuous guidance of a Satguru. Entering the deeper levels of the mind, going through the different layers, and successfully coming out of it is known as *tapas* [austerity]. This, including the final transcendence, is possible only with the unconditional grace of a Satguru.

The mind always has expectations. The very existence of the mind is in expecting. A Mahatma will not comply with the expectations and desires of the mind. In order to experience a Master's pure consciousnesses, this nature of the mind must disappear.

Amma, the Inexhaustible Energy

Questioner: Amma, do You ever want to stop the work that You are doing?

Amma: What Amma does is not work. It is worship. There is only pure love in worship. Therefore, it is not work. Amma is worshipping Her children as God. Children, you are all Amma's God.

Love is not complex. It is simple, spontaneous and, indeed, our essential nature. Therefore, it is not work. As for Amma, this way of personally embracing Her children is the simplest way to express Her love for them and to the entire creation. Work is tiring and it dissipates your energy; whereas love can never be tiring or boring. On the contrary, it keeps filling your heart with more and more energy. Pure love makes you feel as light as a flower. You won't feel any heaviness or burden. Ego creates the burden.

The sun never stops shining; the wind, too, continues to blow in eternity; and the river never stops flowing, saying,

"Enough is enough! I have been doing the same work for ages; now it is time for a change." No, they can never stop. They will continue as long as the world exists, because that is their nature. Likewise, Amma cannot stop giving love to Her children, because She never gets bored of loving Her children.

Boredom occurs only when there is no love. Then you want to keep on changing, changing from one place to another, from one object to another. Whereas, nothing gets old when there is love. Everything remains eternally new and fresh. However, for Amma, the present moment is much more important than what needs to be done tomorrow.

Questioner: Does that mean that You will continue giving *darshan* for years to come?

Amma: As long as these hands can move a little bit and reach out to those who come to Her, and as long as there is a little strength and energy to place Her hands on a crying person's shoulder and caress and wipe their tears, Amma will continue giving darshan. To lovingly caress people, console and wipe their tears, until the end of this mortal frame is Amma's wish.

Amma has been giving darshan for the last 35 years. By the grace of the Paramatman [Supreme Soul], Amma hasn't had to cancel a single darshan or program owing to any physical ailment so far. Amma doesn't worry about the next moment. Love is in the present, happiness is in the present, God is in the present and enlightenment is also in the present. So, why worry about the future unnecessarily? What is happening now is more important than what is going to happen. When the present is so beautiful and so full, why worry about the future? Let the future unfold by itself from the present.

The Lost Son Found

r. Jaggu is a resident of Amma's ashram in India. Recently, his family gave him the money to travel with Amma to Europe. By the time he got his visa cleared, it was late and Amma and Her tour group had already left India. However, we were all happy that Jaggu was going to join us in Antwerp, Belgium.

It was Jaggu's first trip outside India. He had never traveled in an airplane before. So, we made all the arrangements to have him picked up from the airport well in advance. Devotees waited outside the airport with the car, but Jaggu didn't come out. The airport authorities confirmed that a passenger named Jaggu was on the flight from London-Heathrow. They said that he landed at the Brussels International Airport at around 4:00 p.m. Four hours had passed since the flight landed, yet there was no information regarding Dr. Jaggu.

With the help of airport workers, the local devotees elaborately searched all over the airport. The airport paging system announced Jaggu's name several times. There was absolutely no response, and there was no sign of Jaggu anywhere.

Eventually, everyone was forced to believe that Dr. Jaggu had gotten lost somewhere—either in the gigantic airport or in the city of Brussels in a desperate attempt to somehow reach the program.

Meanwhile, Amma was blissfully practicing some new bhajans, calmly sitting in the midst of the entire tour group. As everyone was feeling a bit worried and anxious about Jaggu's unexpected disappearance, I disclosed the news to Amma in the middle of the singing. I expected Her to express an outpouring of motherly concern. But to my astonishment, Amma turned around and simply said, "Come on, sing the next song."

To me, this was a positive sign. Seeing Amma remain as cool as a cucumber, I told the devotees, "I think Jaggu is absolutely safe, because Amma is so calm. Had there been any problem, She definitely would have been more concerned."

Just a few minutes later, Brahmachari Dayamrita appeared and announced, "Jaggu just showed up at the front gate." Almost simultaneously, Dr. Jaggu walked in with a big smile on his small face.

However, as per the adventurous story narrated by Jaggu, he really had gotten lost. He said, "When I got out of the airport, there was nobody there. I didn't know what to do. Though I was a little worried, I had strong faith that Amma would send someone to save me from the totally unfamiliar situation. Fortunately, I had the address of the program venue. One couple took pity on me and helped me reach here."

Amma said, "Amma very well knew you were all right and would find your way here. That is why Amma remained calm when they told Her you were missing."

Later that evening, I asked Amma how She knew that Jaggu was safe. She said, "Amma simply knew."

"But how?" My curiosity was stirred.

Amma said, "Just as you see your own image in a mirror, Amma could see him safe."

I asked, "Did you see Jaggu getting help or did You inspire the couple to assist him?" Amma wouldn't say anything further about it, though I made a couple more attempts.

Violence

Questioner: Amma, can violence and war ever be a means to achieving peace?

Amma: War will not serve as a means to achieving peace. This is an unadulterated truth that history has revealed to us. Unless a transformation takes place in one's consciousness, peace will remain a far cry. Only spiritual thinking and living will bring this transformation. Therefore we will never be able to correct a particular situation by waging war.

Peace and violence are opposites. Violence is strong reaction, not response. Reaction triggers more reactions. This is simple logic. Amma has heard that in England there existed a peculiar way of punishing thieves. Having brought the culprit to a crossroads, they would flog the thief naked in front of a big gathering. The purpose was to let the whole town know of the severe punishment they would receive if they committed a crime. However, soon they had to change this system, as such occasions created a wonderful opportunity for pickpockets. They utilized the time to pick the pockets of those who remained engrossed in the scene. The punishment ground itself became a breeding ground for crime.

Question: Does that mean that there should not be any punishment at all?

Amma: No, no, not at all. As the majority of the world's population does not know how to use freedom in a manner benefiting society, a certain amount of fear—"I will be punished if I don't observe the law"—is good. However, choosing the path of violence and war to establish peace and harmony in society will not have long-lasting effect. This is simply because violence creates deep wounds and hurt feelings in society's mind, which will manifest as stronger violence and conflict at a later stage.

Question: So, what is the solution?

Amma: Do whatever you can to expand your individual consciousness. Only an expanded consciousness is capable of true understanding. Such people alone will be able to change society's outlook. This is why spirituality is so important in today's world.

Ignorance Is the Problem

Questioner: Is there any difference between the problems of people in India and in the West?

Amma: From an external point of view, the problems of the people in India and in the West are different. However, the fundamental problem, the root of all problems, everywhere in the world, is one and the same. That is ignorance, ignorance about the Atman [Self], about our essential nature.

Too much concern about physical security and too little concern about spiritual security is the hallmark of today's world. This focus should change. Amma is not saying that people shouldn't take care of their body and physical existence. No, that is not the point. However, the basic problem is the confusion over what is permanent and what is impermanent. The impermanent, which is the body, is given too much importance, and the permanent, which is the Atman, is completely forgotten. This attitude should change.

Questioner: Do You see possibilities for change in our society?

Amma: Possibilities are always there. The important question is whether society and the individuals are willing to change.

In a classroom all the students get the same opportunity. However, how much a student learns depends on his or her receptivity.

In today's world everyone wants others to change first. It is hard to find people who sincerely feel that they themselves have to undergo a change. Instead of thinking others should change first, each individual should strive to change him- or herself. Unless a transformation takes place in the inner world, things will be more or less the same in the outer world.

Interpreting Humility

To a devotee who asked a question about humility:

Amma: Normally, when we say, "That person is so humble," it simply means "He has supported my ego and helped me to keep it intact, unhurt. I wanted him to do something for me, and he did it without raising any objection. So he is such a humble person." This is what that statement really means. However, the moment the "humble person" opens his mouth and questions us, even if it is for a good reason, our opinion changes. Now we will say, "He is not as humble as I thought." The indication is, "He has hurt my ego, and therefore he is not so humble."

Are We Special?

eporter: Amma, do You think the people of this country are special?

Amma: As for Amma, the entire human race, the entire creation, is very special because divinity is in everyone. Amma sees that divinity in the people here as well. So you all are special.

Self-Help or self-help

Questioner: Self-help methods and self-help books have become quite popular in Western society. Amma, could You please share Your thoughts on this?

Amma: It all depends on how one interprets self-help.

Questioner: What do You mean by that?

Amma: Is it Self-help or self-help?

Questioner: What is the difference?

Amma: Real Self-help is helping your heart to blossom; whereas self-help is strengthening the ego.

Questioner: So, what do You suggest, Amma?

Amma: "Accept the Truth" is what Amma would say.

Questioner: I don't understand.

Amma: That is what the ego does. It won't allow you to accept the Truth or to understand anything in the right way.

Questioner: How do I see Truth?

Amma: To see Truth, you need to see the false first.

Questioner: Is the ego really an illusion?

Amma: Will you accept it if Amma says so?

Questioner: *Hmm…* if You want.

Amma: (laughing) If *Amma* wants? The question is do *you* want to hear and accept the Truth?

Questioner: Yes, I want to hear and accept the Truth.

Amma: Then the Truth is God.

Questioner: That means the ego is unreal; doesn't it?

Amma: The ego is unreal. It is the trouble in you.

Questioner: So, everyone is carrying that trouble everywhere they go?

Amma: Yes, humans are becoming mobile troubles.

Questioner: So, what is the next step?

Amma: If you want to strengthen the ego, then help your self to become stronger. Or if you want Self-help, seek God's help.

Questioner: Many people are afraid to lose their ego. They think that it is the basis for their existence in the world.

Amma: If you really want to seek God's help to discover your True Self, then you need not be afraid of losing your ego, the small self.

Questioner: But then, by strengthening the ego, we have worldly gains, which are direct, immediate experiences. On the contrary, by losing our ego, the experience is not so direct and immediate.

Amma: That is why faith is so important on the path to the True Self. For everything to work properly and produce the right result, the right contact should be established and the right sources should be tapped. As for spirituality, the contact point and the source are within. Touch that point and then you will have direct and immediate experience.

Ego Is Only a Small Flame

Amma: The ego is a very small flame that can be extinguished at any moment.

Questioner: How do You describe ego in this context?

Amma: All that you accumulate—name, fame, money, power, position—fuel nothing but the small flame of the ego, which can be extinguished at any moment. Even the body and mind are part of the ego. They all are impermanent in nature; therefore they too are part of this insignificant flame.

Questioner: But, Amma, these are important things for a normal human being.

Amma: Of course, they are important. That doesn't mean that they are permanent. They are trivial, because they are impermanent. You can lose them at any moment. Time will snatch them away without prior notice. To use and enjoy them is okay, but to consider them permanent is false perception. In other words, understand them to be transient and don't feel too proud of them.

Building your inner connection with the permanent and unchangeable, with God, or the Self, is the most important thing in life. God is the source, the real center of our life and existence. Everything else is the periphery. Real Self-help happens only when you establish your connection with God, the real *bindu* [center], not with the periphery.

Questioner: Amma, do we gain anything by extinguishing this small flame of the ego? On the contrary, we may even lose our identity as an individual.

Amma: Of course, by extinguishing the smaller flame of ego, you will lose your identity as a small, limited individual. Nevertheless, this is absolutely nothing compared to what you gain from that apparent loss—the sun of pure knowledge, the inextinguishable light. Also, when you lose your identity as a small, limited self, you become one with the bigger than the biggest, the universe, the unconditional consciousness. In order for this experience to happen, you need the constant guidance of a *Satguru* [True Master].

Questioner: Losing my identity! Isn't that a scary experience?

Amma: It is only losing one's small self. Our True Self can never be lost. It is scary because you are tremendously identified with your ego. The bigger the ego, the more scared you are and more vulnerable too.

News

*J*ournalist: Amma what is Your opinion about the news and news media?

Amma: Very good, if they discharge their responsibilities to society with honesty and truthfulness. They do a great service to humanity.

Amma has heard a story: Once, a group of men were sent to a forest to work for a year. Two women were appointed to cook for them. At the end of the contract, two workers in the group married the two women. The next day the newspaper carried the hot news: "Two Percent of Men Marry 100 Percent of Women!"

The journalist enjoyed the story and had a good laugh.

Amma: Such reporting is okay if it is for humour, but not for an honest report.

The Chocolate Kiss &
The Third Eye

ne devotee was dozing off as he was trying to meditate. Amma threw a chocolate Kiss at him. Amma has perfect aim. The chocolate hit right on the spot between his eyebrows. The man opened his eyes with a start. With the chocolate in his hand, the man looked around to find out from where it had come. Seeing his plight, Amma burst into laugher. When he realized that Amma had thrown it, the man's face lit up. He touched the chocolate to his forehead, as if bowing to it. But the next moment he laughed aloud, and then got up from his seat and walked up to Amma.

Questioner: The Kiss hit the right spot, between the eyebrows, the spiritual center. Maybe this will help to open my third eye.

Amma: It won't.

Questioner: Why?

Amma: Because you said "maybe"; this means you are doubtful. Your faith is not complete. How can it happen if you have no faith?

Questioner: So are You saying that it would have happened if I had full faith?

Amma: Yes. If you have complete faith, realization can happen at anytime, anywhere.

Questioner: Are You serious?

Amma: Yes, of course.

Questioner: Oh, my God... did I lose a great opportunity!

Amma: Don't worry, be aware and be wakeful. Opportunities will come again. Be patient and keep trying.

The man looked a little disappointed and turned to walk back to his seat.

Amma: (tapping him on his back) By the way, why did you laugh aloud?

Hearing the question the devotee once again broke into laughter.

Questioner: As I dozed through my meditation, I was having a wonderful dream. I saw You throwing a chocolate Kiss to wake me up. I suddenly woke up. It took me a few moments to realize that You really had thrown a chocolate Kiss.

Along with the man, Amma and all the devotees who sat around Her broke into laughter.

The Nature of Enlightenment

Questioner: Are You especially worried or pleased about something?

Amma: The outer Amma is worried about Her children's well being. And as a part of helping Her children grow spiritually, She might sometimes even be pleased or upset with them. However, the inner Amma is unperturbed and detached, abiding in a state of constant bliss and peace. She is not affected by anything that happens externally, as She is fully aware of the big picture.

Questioner: The ultimate state of abidance is described using so many adjectives. For example: unshakeable, firm, immovable, unchangeable, etc. It sounds like it is a solid, rock-like state. Amma, please help me understand better.

Amma: Those words are used to convey the inner state of detachment, the capacity to watch and be a witness to everything—to distance yourself from all circumstances of life.

However, enlightenment is not a rock-like state where one loses all inner feelings. It is a state of mind, a spiritual attainment, into which you can withdraw yourself and remain absorbed whenever you want. After you tap into the infinite source of energy, your capacity to feel and express everything gains a special, unearthly beauty and depth. If an enlightened person wishes, he or she can express emotions in whatever intensity he or she desires.

Sri Rama cried when the demon king, Ravana, kidnapped his holy consort, Sita. In fact, lamenting like a mortal human being, he asked every creature in the forest, "Have you seen my Sita? Where did she go, leaving me alone?" Krishna's eyes were filled with tears when He saw his dear friend Sudama after a very long time. Similar incidents are there in Christ's and Buddha's lives as well. These Mahatmas were as expansive as limitless space and therefore could reflect any emotion they wanted. They were reflective, not reactive.

Questioner: Reflective?

Amma: Like a mirror, Mahatmas respond to situations with perfect spontaneity. Eating when you are hungry is a response. Whereas, eating whenever you see food is a reaction. It is also a disease. Responding to a particular situation, remaining unaffected by it and then moving to the next moment is what a Mahatma does.

Feeling and expressing emotions and honestly sharing them without reservation only adds to an enlightened being's spiritual splendor and glory. It is wrong to see that as a weakness. It should rather be considered as an expression of their compassion and love in a much more human way. Otherwise, how could ordinary humans understand their concern and love?

The Seer

uestioner: What prevents us from experiencing God?

Amma: The feeling of otherness.

Questioner: How can we remove it?

Amma: By becoming more and more aware, more conscious.

Questioner: Conscious of what?

Amma: Conscious of everything that happens inside and outside.

Questioner: How do we become more aware?

Amma: Awareness occurs when you understand that everything the mind projects is meaningless.

Questioner: Amma, the scriptures say that the mind is inert, but You say that the mind projects. This sounds contradictory. How can the mind project if it is inert?

Amma: Just as people, especially children, project different forms in the infinite sky. Looking at the sky, small children will say, "There is a chariot, and there goes a demon. Oh! Look at the radiant face of that celestial being!" and so forth. Does this mean that these forms are really in the sky? No, the children are simply imagining those forms in the vast sky. In reality, it is the clouds that assume different forms. The sky, the infinite space, is just there—all names and forms are superimposed upon it.

Questioner: But if the mind is inert, how can it even superimpose on or cover the Atman?

Amma: Though it seems like the mind is seeing, the real seer is the Atman. The accumulated tendencies, which comprise the mind, are like a pair of glasses. Every person is wearing different colored glasses. Depending on the color of the glasses, we correspondingly see and judge the world. Behind these glasses, the Atman remains still, as a witness, simply illuminating everything by its presence. But we mistake the mind for the Atman. Suppose we wear a pair of pink-tinted sunglasses—don't we see the whole world in pink? Here, who is the real seer? "We" are the real seer, and the pair of glasses is just inert, isn't it?

We won't be able to see the sun if we stand behind a tree. Does this mean that the tree is capable of covering the sun? No, it simply shows the limitations of our eyes and sight. Similar is the feeling that the mind can cover the Atman.

Questioner: If we are of the nature of the Atman, why should we put forth effort to know it?

Amma: Humans have the wrong notion that they can attain everything through effort. Effort, in fact, is the pride in us. In our journey to God, all efforts that stem from ego will crumble and result in failure. This, in fact, is a divine message, the message of the need for surrender and grace. This eventually helps us to realize the limitations of our effort, of our ego. In short, effort teaches us that through effort alone we will not attain our goals. Ultimately, grace is the determining factor.

Whether it is striving for God-realization or for achieving worldly desires, grace is the factor that fulfills the goal.

Innocence Is Divine Shakti

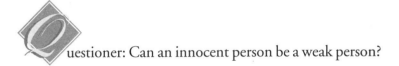

Questioner: Can an innocent person be a weak person?

Amma: "Innocence" is a greatly misinterpreted word. It is even used to refer to non-reactive and timid people. Ignorant and illiterate people also are usually thought of as innocent. Ignorance is not innocence. Ignorance is lack of real love, discrimination and understanding, whereas true innocence is pure love endowed with discrimination and understanding. It is *shakti* [divine energy]. Even in a timid person, there is ego. A truly innocent person is a truly egoless person; therefore he or she is the most powerful person.

Amma Cannot Be Otherwise

Amma (to a devotee during darshan): What are you thinking?

Devotee: I was wondering how You could sit for so long, hours on end, with absolute patience and radiance.

Amma: (laughing) Daughter, how come you think incessantly, in an unbroken manner?

Devotee: It just happens. I cannot be otherwise.

Amma: So, that is the answer: it just happens, Amma cannot be otherwise.

Like Recognizing Your Beloved

man asked Amma a question on the lover-and-beloved attitude of a seeker following the path of devotion.

Amma: Love can happen anywhere at any time. It is like recognizing your beloved in a crowd. You see her standing in a corner with thousands of other people, but your eyes see her and her alone. You recognize her, communicate with her, and you fall in love, isn't it so? You don't think—thinking stops and, suddenly, for a few moments, you are in the heart. You remain in love. In a similar manner, it all happens in a split second. You are right there, in the center of your heart, which is pure love.

Questioner: If that is the real center of love, then what makes us move away and get distracted from that point?

Amma: Possessiveness—in other words, attachment. It kills the beauty of that pure experience. Once attachment overpowers, you go astray, and love becomes misery.

The Feeling of Otherness

Questioner: Will I attain *samadhi* [enlightenment] in this lifetime?

Amma: Why not?

Questioner: If so, what should I do to accelerate the process?

Amma: First of all, forget about samadhi and focus completely on your *sadhana* [spiritual practices] with strong faith. A true *sadhak* [spiritual seeker] believes more in the present than in the future. When we lay our faith in the present moment, all our energy will also be here and now. The result is surrender. Surrender to the present moment, and it will happen.

Everything happens spontaneously when you distance yourself from your mind. Once this happens, then you will remain completely in the present. The mind is the "other" in you. It is the mind that creates the feeling of otherness.

Amma will tell you story: There was once an acclaimed architect. He had several students. With one of them, the architect had a very peculiar relationship. He wouldn't proceed with any work until he'd gotten confirmation from this student. If the student said no to any drawing or sketch, the architect would immediately give it up. The architect would draw sketch after sketch until the student said yes. The architect was obsessed with seeking the opinion of his student. He wouldn't take any step further unless the student said, "Okay, sir, you go ahead with that design now."

Once, they were invited to design a temple door. The architect began drawing different sketches. As usual he showed each and every one of them to his student. The student said no to everything that the architect produced. He worked day and night creating hundreds of new designs. But the student didn't like any of them. Time was running out, and they had to finish very soon. At one point, the architect sent the student out to fill his pen with ink. It took a while for the student to return. Meanwhile the architect was engrossed in designing another model. Just when the student entered the room, the architect finished the new model and, showing it to the student, asked, "How about this?"

"Yes, that is it!" said the excited student.

"Now I know why!" responded the architect. "So far, I was obsessed with your presence and opinion. Because of that I could never be 100 percent present in what I was doing. Now, when you were away, I was free, relaxed and remained surrendered to the moment. That is how it happened."

In reality, it was not the disciple's presence that created the obstruction; it was the architect's attachment to his opinions. Once he could distance himself from that, he was suddenly in the present and a genuine creation took place.

Thinking that samadhi is something that happens in the future, you sit dreaming about it. You dissipate a lot of *shakti* [divine energy] dreaming about samadhi. Channel that shakti properly—use it to focus on the present moment—and meditation, or samadhi, will happen just like that. The goal is not in the future; it is in the present. To be in the present verily is samadhi, and that is true meditation.

Is God Male or Female?

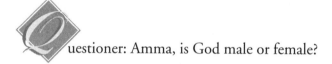 uestioner: Amma, is God male or female?

Amma: God is neither he nor she. God is beyond such limited definitions. God is "It" or "That." But if you need to define God as either he or she, she is better, because she contains he.

Questioner: This answer may irritate men, for it puts women on a higher pedestal.

Amma: Neither men nor women should be placed on a higher pedestal, as God has given both of them an adorable place of their own. Men and women were not made to compete with one another but to complete each other's lives.

Questioner: What do You mean by "complete"?

Amma: It means to support one another and to journey toward perfection together.

Questioner: Amma, don't You think many men feel superior to women?

Amma: Whether it is feeling "I am superior" or "I am inferior," both are products of the ego. If men feel, "We are superior to women," it only shows their over-inflated ego, which certainly is a major weakness and is destructive as well. In a similar manner, if women think that they are inferior to men, it simply means, "We are inferior now, whereas we want to be superior." What else can this be but ego? Both are inappropriate and unhealthy attitudes that will increase the gap between men and women. If we don't bridge the gulf by giving due respect and love to both men and women, the future of humanity will only grow darker.

Spirituality Creates Balance

Questioner: Amma, when You said that God is more a she than a he, You didn't mean the external appearance, did You?

Amma: No, it is not the external appearance. It is the inner realization that matters. There is a woman inside every man and vice versa. The woman in man—that is, the true love and compassion in man—should awaken. This is the significance behind the Ardhanarishwara (half god and half goddess) in the Hindu faith. If the feminine aspect in a woman is asleep, she is not a mother and she is away from God. But if that aspect is awake in a man, he is more of a mother and he is closer to God. This is equally applicable to the masculine aspect as well. The whole purpose of spirituality is to create the proper balance between the masculine and the feminine. Therefore, the inner awakening of consciousness is more important than the external appearance.

Attachment & Love

A middle-aged man was explaining to Amma how sad he felt after his divorce.

Questioner: Amma, I loved her so much and did everything that I could to make her happy. Even then this tragedy has happened in my life. Sometimes I feel devastated. Please help me. What am I supposed to do? How can I get over this pain?

Amma: Son, Amma understands your pain and your suffering. It is difficult to overcome such emotionally depressing situations. However, it is also important to have a proper understanding of what you are experiencing, particularly since it has become a stumbling block in your life.

The most important thing for you to contemplate is whether this sadness comes from real love or from attachment. In real love, there is no self-destructive pain, because you simply love her and don't possess her. Probably, you are too attached to her or you are too possessive. That is where this sadness and depressing thoughts are coming from.

Questioner: Do You have a simple method or technique then to overcome this self-destructive pain?

Amma: "Am I really in love or am I too attached?" Ask yourself this question as deeply as you can. Contemplate on it. And soon you will realize that the love we know is really attachment. Most people are craving for attachment, not real love. So, Amma would say that it is an illusion. In a way, we are betraying ourselves. We mistake attachment for love. Love is the center and attachment is in the periphery. Be in the center and detach yourself from the periphery. Then the pain will go away.

Questioner: (in a confessing tone) You are right. I realize my predominant feeling toward my ex-wife is attachment, not love, as You have explained.

Amma: If you have realized the root cause of the pain, then let go of it and be free. The disease has been diagnosed, the infected part has been found—now remove it. Why do you want to carry this unnecessary burden? Just throw it away.

How to Overcome Life's Dangers

Questioner: Amma, how do I recognize the impending dangers in life?

Amma: By increasing your discriminative power.

Questioner: Is discrimination the same as subtlety of mind?

Amma: It is the capacity of the mind to remain watchful in the present.

Questioner: But, Amma, how does that warn me of the future dangers?

Amma: If you are watchful in the present, you will face less danger in the future. However, you cannot evade or avert all troubles.

Questioner: Does *jyotish* [Vedic astrology] help us to understand the future better and therefore avoid possible dangers?

Amma: Even adepts in that field go through difficult periods in life. There are astrologers who have very little discrimination and intuition. Such people endanger their own lives as well as the lives of others. It is not knowledge of astrology or getting your chart read that steers one clear of life's dangers. It is a deeper understanding of life and a discriminative approach to different situations that really help one to have more peace and fewer problems.

Questioner: Are discrimination and understanding one and the same?

Amma: Yes, they are the same. The more discrimination you have, the more understanding you gain and vice-versa.

The greater capacity you have to be in the present, the more watchful you will become and the more revelations you will have. You will receive more messages from the divine. Every moment brings such messages to you. If you are open and receptive, you can feel them.

Questioner: Amma, are You saying that these revelations will helps us recognize possible future dangers?

Amma: Yes, you will get hints and signals from such revelations.

Questioner: What kinds of hints and signals?

Amma: How do you know that you are going to get a migrane headache? You will feel very uneasy and will start seeing black circles in front of your eyes; won't you? Once the symptoms manifest, you will take the right medicine and it will help. Likewise, before failures or dangers in life, certain signals appear. People usually miss them. However, if you have a clearer and receptive mind, you can feel them and take the necessary steps to overcome them.

Amma has heard the following anecdote: A journalist was interviewing a successful businessman. The reporter asked, "Sir, what is the secret behind your success?"

Businessman: "Two words."

Journalist: "What are they?"

Businessman: "Right decisions."

Journalist: "How do you make right decisions?"

Businessman: "One word."

Journalist: "What is that?"

Businessman: "Experience."

Journalist: "How do you acquire such experience?"

Businessman: "Two words."

Journalist: "What are they?"

Businessman: "Wrong decisions."

So, you see, son, it all depends on how you accept, understand and surrender to situations.

Amma will tell you another story: Invited by Yudhishthira, the Kauravas visited Indraprastha, the royal capital of the Pandavas*. The place was so skillfully engineered that some places looked like beautiful lakes, which in reality were only normal floors. Similarly, there were other spots that, even though they

*The Pandavas and the Kauravas were the two opposing sides that fought in the Mahabharata War.

appeared to be normal floors, in reality were pools filled with water. The whole surrounding had a surreal air to it. As the 100 brothers led by Duryodhana, the eldest Kaurava, walked through the beautiful garden, they almost disrobed to swim, thinking that there was a pool before them. Nevertheless, it was an ordinary floor that only appeared to be a pool. However, before long, all the brothers, including Duryodhana, fell into a real pool that appeared like an ordinary floor and got completely drenched. Panchali, the wife of the five brothers, burst into laughter seeing this hilarious scene. Duryodhana and his brothers felt greatly insulted by this.

This was one of the key incidents that triggered a lot of anger and desire for revenge in the Kaurava brothers, which later led to the Mahabharata War and enormous destruction.

This story is very significant. In real life too, we face many situations that appear really dangerous, and so we take a number of precautionary steps when facing them. However, eventually they may turn out to be harmless. And other circumstances that seem safe may ultimately be very precarious. Nothing is insignificant. That is why it is important that we have *shraddha* [sharp discrimination, alertness and awareness] when facing life and the varied experiences that it brings.

Do Not Hoard God's Wealth

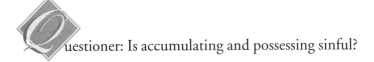

Questioner: Is accumulating and possessing sinful?

Amma: It is not sinful as long as you are compassionate. In other words, you must have the willingness to share with the poor and needy.

Questioner: Otherwise?

Amma: Otherwise it is a sin.

Questioner: Why?

Amma: Because all that is here is God's. Our ownership is temporary; it comes and goes.

Questioner: But doesn't God want us to use all He has created for us?

Amma: Of course, but God doesn't want us to misuse these things. God also wants us to use our discrimination while enjoying all He has created.

Questioner: What is discrimination?

Amma: Discrimination is applying knowledge in such a way that it doesn't mislead you. In other words, using knowledge to distinguish between dharma and *adharma* [righteousness and unrighteousness], the permanent and the impermanent is discrimination.

Questioner: How then do we use the objects of the world with discrimination?

Amma: Renounce ownership—consider all things as God's and enjoy them. This world is is a temporary stop. You are here for a short period, as a visitor. Due to your ignorance, you divide everything, every inch of land, as yours and theirs. The piece of land you claim as your own has belonged to many others before. Now the previous owners are buried in it. Today, it may be your turn to play the role of owner, but remember, one day you too will disappear. Then another person will come and fill your shoes. So, is there any meaning in claiming ownership?

Questioner: What role am I supposed to play here?

Amma: Be God's servant. God, the giver of everything, wants you to share His wealth with everyone. If that is God's will, then who are you to keep it for yourself? If, against God's will, you refuse to share it, then it is hoarding, which is equal to stealing. Just have the attitude of a visitor to this world.

Once, a man came to see a Mahatma. Finding no furniture or decorative pieces in the house, the man asked the great soul, "Strange, why is there no furniture here?"

"Who are you?" the Mahatma asked him.

"I am a visitor," replied the man.

"So am I," said the Mahatma. "Therefore, why should I go about unintelligently accumulating things?"

Amma & Nature

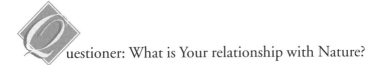

Questioner: What is Your relationship with Nature?

Amma: Amma's connection with Nature is not a relationship; it is total Oneness. A lover of God is a lover of Nature as well, because God and Nature are not two. Once you attain the state of enlightenment, you become connected to the whole universe. In Amma's relationship with Nature, there is no lover or beloved—love alone is. There are not two; there is only one; there is only love.

Normally relationships lack real love. In relationships of ordinary love, there are two—or you could say that there are three—the lover, the beloved and love. In real love, however, the lover and beloved disappear, and what remains is an unbroken experience of pure, unconditional love.

Questioner: What is Nature to human beings?

Amma: Nature means life to humans. She is part and parcel of our existence. It is an interrelationship that goes on at every moment and on every level. Not only are we totally dependent on Nature, but we affect her and she affects us. And when we truly love Nature, she responds in kind and opens up her endless resources to us. And just as when we truly love another person, in our love toward Nature we should be infinitely faithful, patient and compassionate.

Questioner: Is this relationship an exchange or is it a mutual support?

Amma: It is both and even more. However, Nature will continue to exist even without human beings. She knows how to take care of herself. But humans require the support of Nature for their existence.

Questioner: What happens if the exchange between Nature and human beings become complete?

Amma: She will stop hiding things from us. Opening her infinite treasure of natural wealth, she will allow us to enjoy it. Like a mother, she will protect us, nurture and nourish us.

In a perfect relationship between humanity and Nature, a circular energy field is created in which both start flowing into each other. To put it in another way, when we human beings fall in love with Nature, she will fall in love with us.

Questioner: What is it that makes people act so cruelly to Nature? Is it selfishness or lack of understanding?

Amma: It is both. In fact, it is lack of understanding that manifests as selfish actions.

Basically, it is ignorance. Due to ignorance, people think that Nature is just a place from which they can keep on taking without giving. Most human beings know only the language of exploitation. Due to their utter selfishness, they are unable to consider their fellow beings. In today's world, our relationship with Nature is nothing but an extension of the selfishness that we feel within.

Questioner: Amma, what do You mean by considering others?

Amma: What Amma means is to consider others with compassion. In order to consider others—Nature or human beings—the first and foremost quality that one needs to develop is a deep inner connection, a connection with one's own conscience. Conscience, in the real sense, is the power to see others as yourself. Just as you see your own image in a mirror, you see others as you. You reflect others, their feelings, both happiness and sorrow. We have to develop this capacity in our relationship with Nature.

Questioner: The original inhabitants of this country were Native Americans. They worshipped nature and had a deep connection with her. Do You think that is what we also should do?

Amma: What each one should do depends on their mental constitution. However, Nature is a part of life, a part of the whole. Nature is verily God. Worshipping Nature is the same as worshipping God.

By worshipping Mount Govardhana, Lord Krishna taught us a great lesson: to make Nature worship part of our daily life. He asked his people to worship Mount Govardhana because it protected them. Similarly Lord Rama, before building the bridge across the sea, did three days of severe penance to please the ocean. Even Mahatmas give so much respect and regard for Nature and seek her blessings prior to commencing any action. In India, there are temples for birds, animals, trees and even for lizards and poisonous snakes. This is to emphasize the great significance of the connection between humans and Nature.

Questioner: Amma, in order to re-establish the relationship between human beings and Nature, what is Your advice?

Amma: Let us be compassionate and considerate. Let us take from Nature only what we really need, and then try to return it to some extent. For only by giving will we receive. A blessing is something that comes back to us in response to the way we approach something. If we approach Nature with love, considering her as life, as God, as part of our own existence, then she will serve as our best friend, a friend whom we can always trust, a friend who would never betray us. But if our attitude toward Nature is wrong, then, instead of Nature responding with a blessing, the result will be a negative reaction. Nature will turn against the human race if we are not careful in our relationship with her, and the consequences may be disastrous.

Many of God's beautiful creations have already been lost due to people's misbehavior and total disregard for Nature. If we continue to act this way, it will only pave the way for disaster.

Sannyas, The Peak of Human Existence

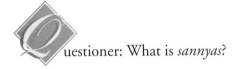

Questioner: What is *sannyas*?

Amma: Sannyas is the peak of human existence. It is the fulfillment of human birth.

Questioner: Is sannyas a state of mind, or is it something else?

Amma: Sannyas is both a state of mind and a state of "no mind."

Questioner: Amma, how do You explain that state… or whatever it is?

Amma: When even worldly experiences are difficult to explain, how can sannyas, the highest form of experience, be explained? It is a state wherein one has complete freedom of choice internally.

Questioner: Amma, I know that I am asking too many questions, but what do You mean by "internal freedom of choice"?

Amma: Human beings are slaves to their thoughts. The mind is nothing but a constant flow of thoughts. The pressure created by these thoughts makes you a helpless victim to outside situations. There are countless thoughts and emotions, both subtle and gross, in a person. Unable to look closely and discriminate between the good ones and the bad ones, the productive and the destructive, most people fall easy prey to harmful impulses and become identified with negative emotions. In the supreme state of sannyas, one has the choice of identifying with or remaining detached from each particular emotion and thought. You have the choice to cooperate or not to cooperate with each thought, emotion and given situation. Even if you chose to identify, you have the option to withdraw and move forward at any time you want. This, indeed, is complete freedom.

Questioner: What is the meaning of the ochre cloth that *sannyasins* wear?

Amma: It indicates the inner attainment or the goal you desire to reach. It also means that you are no more interested in worldly achievements—an open declaration that your life is dedicated to God and the realization of the Self. It means that your body and mind are consumed by the fire of *vairagya* [detachment] and that you don't belong to any particular nation, caste, creed, sect or religion anymore. However, sannyas is not just about wearing colored clothes.

The cloth is only a symbol, indicating a state of being, the transcendental state. Sannyas is an inner change in your attitudes toward life and how you perceive it. You become totally egoless. Now, you no longer belong to yourself, but to the world, and your life has become an offering to the service of humanity. In that state you do not ever expect or demand anything from anyone. In the state of true sannyas, you become more of a presence than a personality.

During the ceremony, when the disciple receives sannyas from the Master, the disciple cuts the small tuft of hair that he has always worn from the back of his head. The disciple then offers both the tuft and his sacred thread* into the sacrificial fire. This is symbolic of giving up all attachments to the body, mind and intellect, and to all enjoyments here and hereafter.

Sannyasins are supposed to either grow their hair long or completely shave it. In olden times, sannyasins would grow their hair in matted locks. This shows detachment to the body. You are no longer interested in beautifying the body, because the real beauty lies in knowing the Atman. The body is changing, perishing. What is the point in becoming unnecessarily attached to it when your true nature is the changeless and immortal Self?

Attaching oneself to the transient is the cause of all sorrows and sufferings. A sannyasin is one who has realized this great truth—the transient nature of the outside world and the intransient nature of consciousness, which gives beauty and charm to everything.

True sannyas is not something that can be given, rather it is a realization.

Question: Does that mean that it is an attainment?

Amma: You are asking the same question again. Sannyas is the culmination of all the preparations known as *sadhana* [spiritual practices].

Look, we can only attain something that is not ours, something that is not part of us. The state of sannyas is the very core of our existence, that which we really are. Until you realize it,

---

Comprised of three threads, the yajnopavitam is worn across the body to represent the responsibilities one has toward family, society and Guru.

you may call it an attainment, but once true knowledge dawns, you understand that it is the real you and that you were never away from it—that you never could be.

This capacity to know what we really are resides within everyone. We are in a forgetful state. Somebody should remind us of this infinite power within.

For example, there is a person who earns his livelihood by begging in the streets. One day, a stranger comes up to him and says, "Hey, what are you doing here? You are neither a beggar nor a Gypsy-like wanderer. You are a multimillionaire."

The beggar doesn't believe the stranger and walks away, ignoring him completely. But the stranger is lovingly persistent. So he follows the beggar and tells him, "Trust me. I am your friend, and I want to help you. What I am telling you is the truth. You are, indeed, a rich man, and the treasure that you own is, in fact, very near to you."

Now the beggar's curiosity is aroused, so he asks, "Very near to me? Where?"

"Right inside the hut where you live," replies the stranger. "A little digging is enough for it to become yours forever."

Now the beggar doesn't want to waste even a moment. He immediately returns home and digs out the treasure.

The stranger represents the True Master, who gives us the right information and convinces, persuades and inspires us to dig out the priceless treasure that lies latent within us. We are in a forgetful state. The Guru helps us to know who we really are.

There Is Only One Dharma

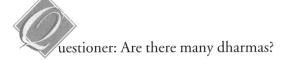

Questioner: Are there many dharmas?

Amma: No, there is only one dharma.

Questioner: But people talk of different dharmas?

Amma: That is because they don't see the one reality. They see only the many, the diverse names and forms.

However, depending on each one's *vasanas* [tendencies], there is more than one dharma, so to speak. For example, a musician may say that music is his or her dharma. Likewise, a businessman could say that doing business is his dharma. And that is okay. However, one cannot find complete fulfillment in any of these. That which gives absolute satisfaction or contentment is real dharma. Whatever one does, unless one is content with oneself, peace will elude them and the feeling "something is missing" will persist. Nothing, no worldly achievement, will fill this empty space in a person's life. Everyone will have to find his or her center within for this feeling of fulfillment to dawn. This is the real dharma. Until then, you will go round and round, in circles, in search of peace and joy.

Questioner: If one follows dharma unfailingly, will it bring both material prosperity and spiritual growth?

Amma: Yes, if one follows dharma in its truest sense, it will definitely help you gain both.

Ravana, the demon king, had two brothers, Kumbhakarna and Vibhishana. When Ravana kidnapped Sita, the holy consort of Lord Rama, both the brothers repeatedly warned Ravana of the disastrous consequences that it could bring and advised him to return Sita to Rama. He completely ignored all their pleadings and eventually declared war against Rama. Though he was aware of the unrighteous attitude of his elder brother, Kumbhakarna finally yielded to Ravana, due to his attachment to him and to his love for the demon race.

Vibhishana, on the other hand, was a very pious and devout soul. He was not able to accept the *adharmic* [unrighteous] ways of his brother and continued expressing his concerns, trying to change his brother's attitude. However Ravana never accepted, considered or even listened to his views. Eventually, the extremely egoistic Ravana got so angry with his youngest brother that he exiled him from the country for his persistence. Vibhishana took refuge at Rama's feet. In the war that followed, Ravana and Kumbhakarna were killed and Sita was regained. Before his return to Ayodhya, Rama's homeland, Rama crowned Vibhishana the king of Lanka.

Of all of the three brothers, Vibhishana was the only one who could create a balance between his worldly and spiritual dharmas. How could he do this? It was the result of his spiritual outlook even while performing his worldly responsibilities, not the other way around. This way of discharging worldly duties will take one to the state of ultimate fulfillment. On the contrary, the other two brothers, Ravana and Kumbhakarna, had a worldly outlook even while performing their spiritual dharma.

Vibhishana's attitude was selfless. He did not ask Rama to make him the king. He only wanted to be firmly rooted in dharma. But that unshakeable vow and determination bestowed all blessings upon him. He attained both material and spiritual prosperity.

Questioner: Amma, that was beautiful. However, true spiritual seekers don't crave for material prosperity, do they?

Amma: No, a sincere seeker's one and only dharma is enlightenment. He or she will be satisfied with nothing less than that experience. Everything else is immaterial for such a person.

Questioner: Amma, I have one more question. Do You think there are Ravanas and Kumbhakarnas in today's world? If so, will it be easy for Vibhishanas to survive in society?

Amma: (laughing) There is a Ravana and Kumbhakarna in everyone. The difference is only in degree. Of course, people with extreme demonic qualities such as Ravana and Kumbhakarna are also there. In fact, all the chaos and conflict that is seen in the present-day world is nothing but the sum total of such minds. However, true Vibhishanas will survive, because they will take refuge in Rama, or God, who will protect them.

Questioner: Though I said that was going to be my last question, I actually have one more, if Amma permits.

Amma: (in English) Okay, ask.

Questioner: Personally, what do You think about these modern-day Ravanas?

Amma: They too are Amma's children.

Unified Action as Dharma

"In this Kaliyuga [Dark Age of Materialism], the general tendency of people all over the world is to move away from each other. They live isolated like islands, with no inner connection. This is dangerous and will only increase the density of the darkness that surrounds us. Whether it is between people or between humans and nature, it is love that creates the bridge, the connection. Unified action is the strength of today's world. So, that should be considered as one of the predominant *dharmas* [duties] of this period."

Devotion & Awareness

Questioner: Is there any connection between awareness and devotion?

Amma: Pure devotion is unconditional love. Unconditional love is surrender. Complete self-surrender means to be fully open or expansive. That openness or expansiveness is awareness. That indeed is Godhood.

Helping the Disciple's Closed Heart to Open

Questioner: Amma, You tell Your devotees and disciples that a personal Guru is very much necessary to attain God, but You considered the entire creation as Your Guru. Don't You think that others have that option too?

Amma: Of course, they do. But on the spiritual path, options usually don't work.

Questioner: In Your case, it worked, didn't it?

Amma: In Amma's case, it wasn't an option. Rather it was simply spontaneous.

Look, my son, Amma doesn't force anything on anyone. For those who have the unshakeable faith to see every single situation, both negative and positive, as a message from God, an external Guru is not necessary. But how many people have that determination and strength?

The path to God is not something that can be forced. That doesn't work. On the contrary, forcing may even ruin the whole process. In this path, the Guru must be immensely patient with the disciple. Just as a bud opens into a beautiful fragrant flower, the Guru helps the disciple's closed heart to fully open.

The disciples are ignorant and the Guru is awakened. The disciples have no idea about the Guru and the plane from which he or she functions. Owing to their ignorance, the disciples can, at times, become extremely impatient. Judgmental as they are, they may even find fault with the Guru. In such circumstances, the unconditional love and compassion of a Perfect Master alone can truly help the disciple.

Meaning of Thankfulness

Questioner: What does it mean to be thankful to the Master, or God?

Amma: It is a humble, open and prayerful attitude that helps you receive God's grace. A True Master has nothing to gain or lose. Established in the supreme state of detachment, the Master is unaffected whether you are thankful or not. However, the attitude of thankfulness helps you to be receptive to God's grace. Thankfulness is an inner attitude. Be thankful to God, because that is the best way to come out of the narrow world created by the body and mind, and to enter the expansive inner world.

The Power Behind the Body

Questioner: Is each soul different, having a separate individual existence?

Amma: Is electricity different, though it manifests differently through fans, refrigerators, televisions and other appliances?

Questioner: No, but do souls have a separate existence after death?

Amma: Depending on their karma [effects of accumulated past actions] and accumulated *vasanas* [tendencies] they will have a seemingly separate existence.

Questioner: Do our individual souls have desires even in that state?

Amma: Yes, but they cannot fulfill them. Just as someone who is completely paralyzed is unable to get up and take things as he likes, such souls are not able to satisfy their desires, as they don't have a body.

Questioner: How long do they stay like that?

Amma: It depends on the intensity of their *prarabdha karma* [the currently manifesting results of past actions].

Questioner: What happens after that is exhausted?

Amma: They will be born again, and the cycle continues until they realize who they really are.

Due to our identification with our body and mind, we think, "I am the doer, I am the thinker," and so on and so forth. In reality, without the presence of the Atman [Self], neither the body nor the mind can function. Can any machine work without electricity? Isn't it the power of electricity that moves everything? Without that power, even a gigantic machine is nothing but a huge pile of iron or steel. Similarly, no matter what or who we are, it is the presence of the Atman that helps us do everything. Without it, we are just dead matter. Forgetting the Atman and becoming mere worshippers of the body is like ignoring the electricity and falling in love with the piece of equipment.

Two Vital Experiences

Questioner: Can Perfect Masters choose the times and circumstances of their births and deaths?

Amma: Only a perfect being has total control over those situations. All others are completely helpless during these two vital experiences. No one will ask you where you want to be born, or who or what you want to be. Similarly, you won't receive any message asking you if you are ready to die.

Both the person who had been constantly complaining about his small one-room apartment and the person who enjoyed the luxury of his mansion will remain silent and comfortable within the small space of a coffin when the presence of the Atman [Self] is no more. A person who couldn't live without air-conditioning even for a second will have absolutely no problem when his or her body is being consumed in the funeral pyre. Why? Because now it is nothing but an inert object.

Questioner: Death is a frightening experience, isn't it?

Amma: It is frightening for those who live their lives completely identified with the ego, without giving any thought to the reality that is beyond the body and mind.

Considering Others

One devotee wanted to have an uncomplicated, easily understandable, short explanation for spirituality.

Amma said, "Compassionately considering others is spirituality."

"Fantastic," said the man and he got up to leave. Amma suddenly caught hold of his hand, saying, "Sit down."

The man obeyed. Holding the devotee who was having *darshan* with one hand, Amma leaned close to him and softly asked him in English, "Story?"

The man was a little perplexed. "Amma, do You want me to tell a story?"

Amma laughed and responded, "No, do you want to hear a story?"

The excited man replied, "I certainly want to hear Your story. I am so blessed."

Amma proceeded to tell the story:

"One day while a man was sleeping with his mouth wide open, a fly flew in. And ever since, the man always felt the fly living inside him.

"As his imagination about the fly grew, the poor fellow began to worry more and more. Soon his worry culminated into intense suffering and depression. He couldn't eat or sleep. There was no joy in his life. His thoughts were always focused on the fly. He could always be seen chasing the fly from one part of his body to another.

"He went to medical doctors, psychologists and psychiatrists and a variety of others to help him get rid of the fly. Everyone said, 'Look, you are alright. There is no fly inside you. Even if a fly went in, it would have died long back. Stop worrying; you are fine.'

"However, the man didn't believe any of them and continued to suffer. One day, a close friend of his took him to a Mahatma. Having listened to his fly story with great attention, the Mahatma examined the man and said, 'You are right. There is, in fact, a fly inside of you. I see it moving around.'

"Still looking into his wide-opened mouth, the Master said, 'Oh, my God! Look at that! It has grown big over the months.'

"The moment the Mahatma uttered these words, the man turned toward his friend and wife and said, 'You see, those fools didn't know anything. This fellow here understands me. Within no time he detected the fly.'

"The Mahatma said, 'Don't move at all. Even the slightest movement can disturb the whole process.' Then he covered the man from head to toe with a thick blanket. 'This will make the process faster. I want to make the whole body, and even inside the body, dark so that the fly is not able to see anything. So don't even open your eyes.'

"The man had already developed such strong faith in the Mahatma that he was 100 percent willing to do whatever the Mahatma said.

"'Now relax and be still.' Saying so, the Mahatma went into another room, his intention being to catch a live fly. Eventually, he managed to catch one and came back with it in a bottle.

"He began to gently move his hands on the patient's body. As he did so, the Mahatma gave a running commentary on the movements of the fly. He said, 'Okay, now don't move, the fly is now sitting on your stomach.... Before I could do anything, it flew up and sat on top of the lungs. I almost caught it.... Oh no, it again escaped! ... Oh my, he is fast! ... Now he is on the stomach again.... Okay, now I am going to chant a mantra that will make the fly motionless.'

"Then he pretended that he was catching the fly and taking it out of the man's stomach. In a few more seconds, the Mahatma asked the man to open his eyes and remove the blanket. When he did that, the Mahatma showed him the fly that was already caught and put in the bottle.

"The man was overjoyed. He began dancing. He told his wife, 'I told you a hundred times that I was right and those psychologists were fools. Now I am going straight to them. I want all my money back!'

"In reality, there was no fly. The only difference was the Mahatma considered the man; the others didn't. They said the truth, but they didn't help him. Whereas, the Mahatma supported him, sympathized with him, understood him and showed him real compassion. This helped the man to overcome his weakness.

"He had a deeper understanding of the man, his suffering and his mental condition, so he came down to his level. On the contrary, the others remained in their level of understanding and didn't consider the patient."

Amma paused and then continued, "Son, this is the whole process of spiritual realization. The Master considers the disciple's fly of ignorance—the ego—as true. Just by considering the disciple and his ignorance, the Master gains the disciple's complete cooperation. Without the cooperation of the disciple, the Master cannot do anything. However, a really inquisitive disciple will not have any problem cooperating with a Genuine Master, as the Master fully considers the disciple and his or her weaknesses before helping the disciple to wake to reality. The real job of a True Master is to help the disciple to also become a master of all situations."

Womb of Love

Questioner: I recently read in a book that we all have a spiritual womb. Does such a thing exist?

Amma: It could only be an example. There is no such visible organ known as the "spiritual womb." Perhaps it means the receptivity that we should develop to feel and experience love within. God has provided each woman with the gift of a womb, where she can carry a child, nurture it, nourish it and finally give birth to it. In a similar manner, we should create enough space within for love to form and grow. Our meditations, prayers and chants will nurture and nourish this love, gradually helping the child of love to grow and expand beyond all limitations. Pure love is *shakti* [energy] in its purest form.

Are Spiritual People Special?

uestioner: Amma, do You think spirituality and spiritual people are special?

Amma: No.

Questioner: Then?

Amma: Spirituality is all about leading a completely normal life in tune with our Inner Self. So, there is nothing special about it.

Questioner: Are You saying that only spiritual-minded people are leading normal lives?

Amma: Did Amma say that?

Questioner: Not directly, but Your statement implies that, doesn't it?

Amma: That is your interpretation of Amma's words.

Questioner: Okay, but what do You think of the majority of people, who live in the world?

Amma: Not the majority, aren't we all living in the world?

Questioner: Amma, please....

Amma: As long we live in the world, we all are worldly people. However, what makes you spiritual is the way you look at life and its experiences while living in the world. See, my son, everyone thinks that they are leading a normal life. Whether they are leading a normal life or not is something that each individual should find out through proper introspection. We should also know that spirituality is not something unusual or extraordinary. Spirituality is not to become special, but to become humble. It is also important to understand that human birth in itself is very special.

Just a Temporary Stop

Questioner: Amma, why is detachment so important in spiritual life?

Amma: Not only spiritual aspirants, but anyone who desires to increase their potential and mental peace must practice detachment. To be detached means to become a *sakshi* [witness] to all life's experiences.

Attachment is loading the mind and detachment is unloading the mind. The more loaded the mind, the more tense it will be and the more it will desire to be unloaded. In today's world, people's minds are becoming more and more loaded with negative thoughts. This will naturally invoke a strong urge, a genuine need for detachment.

Questioner: Amma, I really want to practice detachment, but my conviction always wavers.

Amma: Conviction only comes with awareness. The more awareness you have, the more convinced you will be. Son, consider the world as a temporary stop, a little longer one. We all are traveling, and this is yet another place we are visiting. As on a trip in a bus or train, we will meet many fellow passengers with whom we may talk and share our thoughts on life and world affairs. After a little while, we may even develop an attachment toward the person sitting next to us. However, each of the passengers will have to alight upon reaching their respective destinations. So, the moment you meet a person or settle in a place, maintain the awareness that one day you will have to part. If developed and coupled with a positive attitude, this awareness will certainly guide you in all circumstances of life.

Questioner: Amma, are You saying that one should practice detachment while living in the world?

Amma: (smiling) Where else can you learn detachment, if it is not while living in the world? After death? In reality, practicing detachment is the way to overcome the fear of death. It guarantees a totally pain-free and blissful death.

Questioner: How is that possible?

Amma: Because when you are detached, you remain a sakshi even for the experience of death. Detachment is right attitude. It is correct perception. While watching a movie, if we identify with the characters and later try to imitate them in our life, will that be good or bad? Watch a movie with the awareness that it is only a movie; then you will really enjoy it. The real path to peace is spiritual thinking and a spiritual way of living.

You don't bathe in a river forever; you bathe in it to come out fresh and clean. Likewise, if you are interested in leading a spiritual life, consider your life as a householder as a way to exhaust your *vasanas* [tendencies]. In other words, remember that you are living a family life not to become increasingly immersed in it but to exhaust that and other related vasanas and to become free from the bondage of action. Your aim should be exhaustion of negative vasanas, not their accumulation.

What the Mind Hears

Questioner: Amma, how do You define "mind"?

Amma: It is an instrument that never hears what is told, but only what it wants to hear. You are told one thing, and the mind hears something else. Then, through a series of cutting, editing and pasting, it performs a surgery on what it heard. In this process, the mind removes some things and adds certain other things to the original, interpreting and polishing it until at last it fits you. Then you convince yourself that this is what you were told.

There is a young boy who comes with his parents to the ashram. One day his mother told Amma an interesting incident that happened at home. The mother told her son to be a little more serious about his studies, as his examinations were fast-approaching. The boy's priorities were different. He wanted to play sports and watch movies. In an argument that followed, the boy finally told his mother, "Mom, haven't you heard Amma emphasizing in Her talks to live in the present? For heaven's sake, I don't understand why you are so worried about the examinations, which have yet to come, when I have other things to do in the present." That is what he heard.

Love & Fearlessness

o illustrate how love takes away all fear, Amma told the following story.

Amma: Long ago, there was a king who ruled an Indian state and who lived in a fort on top of a mountain. Every day, a woman used to come to the fort to sell milk. She would arrive around six in the morning and leave the fort before six in the evening. Exactly at six p.m. the huge doors at the entrance of the fort would close, and after that no one could enter or exit until the doors opened again in the morning.

Every morning when the guards opened the huge iron doors, the woman would be standing there, carrying a milk pail on her head.

One evening, by the time the woman made it to the entrance, it was a few seconds past six and the doors had just closed. She had a little boy at home who would be waiting for his mother to return. The woman fell at the feet of the guards and pleaded with them to let her out. With tears in her eyes, she said, "Please take pity on me. My little boy will not eat or sleep unless I am with him. Poor child; he will be crying the whole night without seeing his mother. Please! Let me go!" However, the guards wouldn't budge, for they couldn't act against orders.

The woman ran around the fort in a panic, desperately trying to find a spot where she could get out. She couldn't bear the thought of her innocent little boy anxiously waiting in vain for her to return.

The fort was surrounded by rocky mountains, forests full of thorny bushes, creepers and poisonous plants. As night fell, the mother in the milkmaid grew more restless, and her determination to be with her child intensified. She went round the fort to find a place from where she could climb down and somehow reach her house. Finally, she spotted a place that looked comparatively less steep and deep. After hiding the milk pot in a bush, she cautiously began to descend the mountain. In that process, several parts of her body got cut and bruised. Oblivious of all adversities, the thoughts of her son kept her going. Eventually she succeeded and reached the bottom of the mountain. The milkmaid rushed to her house and spent the night happily with her son.

The next morning, when the guards opened the doors to the fort, they were astonished to see the woman who hadn't been able to leave the previous evening standing outside, waiting to get in.

"If an ordinary milkmaid managed to climb down from our unconquerable fort, there must be a spot where enemies can gain access and attack us," they thought. Realizing the gravity of the situation, the security guards immediately arrested the woman and brought her to the king.

The king was a person of great understanding and maturity. His wisdom, valor and noble nature were praised by the people of the land. He received the milkmaid with great courtesy. With his palms joined in salutation, he said, "Oh mother, if my guards are speaking the truth about you having escaped from here last night, would you be kind enough to show me the place where you managed to climb down?"

The milkmaid led the king, his ministers and the guards to a certain spot. There she retrieved the milk pot that she had hidden in the bush the night before and showed it to the king. Looking down the steep mountainside, the king asked her, "Mother, could you please show us how you managed to climb down here last night?

The milkmaid looked down the sheer, forbidding wall of the mountain and trembled with fear. "No, I can't do it!" she cried.

"Then how did you do it last night?" the king asked.

"I don't know," she replied.

"But I know," the king gently said. "It was your love for your son that gave you the strength and the courage to do the impossible."

In true love, one goes beyond the body, mind and all fears. The power of pure love is infinite. Such love is all-embracing, all-pervading. In that love, one can experience the oneness of the Self. Love is the breathing of the soul. No one will say, "I will breathe only in the presence of my wife, children, parents and friends. I cannot breathe in the presence of my enemies, those who hate me or those who have abused me." You cannot be alive then; you will die. Likewise, love is a presence, beyond all differences. It is present everywhere. It is our life-force.

Pure, innocent love makes everything possible. When your heart is filled with the pure energy of love, even the most impossible task is as easy as picking up a flower.

Why Are There Wars?

Questioner: Amma, why is there so much war and violence?

Amma: Due to lack of understanding.

Questioner: What is lack of understanding?

Amma: Absence of compassion.

Questioner: Are understanding and compassion related?

Amma: Yes, when real understanding arises, you learn to truly consider the other person, overlooking his or her weaknesses. From that, love evolves. As pure love dawns within, compassion does too.

Questioner: Amma, I have heard You say that ego is the cause of war and conflict.

Amma: That is right. Immature ego and lack of understanding are almost the same. We use so many different words, but basically they all mean the same thing.

When humans lose contact with their Inner Self and become more identified with their ego, there can only be violence and war. This is what is happening in today's world.

Questioner: Amma, do You mean that people give too much importance to the external world?

Amma: Civilization [external comforts and development] and *samskara* [practicing enriching thoughts and qualities] are supposed to go hand-in-hand. But what do we see in society? Rapidly degenerating spiritual values, isn't it so? Conflict and war are the lowest point of existence, and the highest is samskara.

The condition of today's world can best be depicted through the following example. Imagine a very narrow road. Two drivers hit the breaks of their cars as the vehicles come very close to each other. Unless one of them backs up and yields way to the other, they cannot go. However, sitting firmly in their seats, the drivers obstinately declare that they are not going to budge even an inch. The situation can be solved only if one of them shows some humility and willingly yields to the other. Then both of them can easily drive to their destinations. The one who yields to the other can also have the joy of knowing that it is only because of them that the other person was able to go.

How Can We Make Amma Happy?

Questioner: Amma, how can I serve You?

Amma: By serving others selflessly.

Questioner: What can I do to make You happy?

Amma: Help others feel happy. That, indeed, makes Amma happy.

Questioner: Amma, don't You want anything from me?

Amma: Yes, Amma wants you to be happy.

Questioner: Amma, You are so beautiful.

Amma: But that beauty is in you also. You just have to find it.

Questioner: I love you, Amma.

Amma: Daughter, in reality, you and Amma are not two. We are one. So there is only love.

The Real Problem

Questioner: Amma, You say that everything is One. But I see everything as separate. Why is it so?

Amma: Seeing things as separate or different is not a problem. The real problem is not being able to behold the Oneness behind that diversity. That is wrong perception, which is indeed a limitation. Your way of looking at the world and what is happening around you needs correcting; after that, everything will automatically change.

Just as our vision requires correcting when our external eyes weaken—that is, when we begin seeing objects as double—the inner eye also needs adjusting, as instructed by someone established in the experience of that Oneness, a *Satguru* [True Master].

Nothing Wrong With the World

Questioner: What is wrong with the world? Things don't look very good. Can we do something about it?

Amma: There is no problem with the world. The problem is with the human mind—the ego. It is uncontrolled ego that makes the world problematic. A little more understanding and a little more compassion can create a lot of change.

Ego rules the world. People are helpless victims of their egos. Sensitive people endowed with compassionate hearts are hard to find. Find your own inner harmony, the beautiful song of life and love within. Go out and serve the suffering. Learn to place others in front of yourself. But in the name of loving and serving others, don't fall in love with your own ego. Keep your ego, but be a master of your own mind and ego. Consider everyone, because that is the doorway to God and to your own Self.

Why Follow the Spiritual Path?

Questioner: Why should one follow the spiritual path?

Amma: This is like the seed asking, "Why should I go beneath the soil, sprout and grow upward?"

Handling Spiritual Energy

Questioner: At least a small number of people lose their sanity after doing spiritual practices. Why does this happen?

Amma: Spiritual practices prepare your limited body and mind to contain the universal *shakti* [energy]. They open the gateway to higher conciousness in you. In other words, they directly deal with pure shakti. If you are not careful, they can cause mental and physical problems. For example, light helps us to see. But too much light will damage our eyes. Similarly, shakti, or bliss, is highly beneficial. However, if you don't know how to handle it in the right manner, it can be dangerous. Only a *Satguru's* [True Master] guidance will truly assist you in this.

An Innocent Heart's Complaint & Compassion

A little boy came running to Amma and showed Her his right palm. Amma affectionately held his finger and asked in English, "What, baby?" He turned around and said, "There...."

Amma: (in English) There, what?

Little boy: Daddy....

Amma: (in English) Daddy, what?

Little boy: (pointing to his palm) Daddy sit here.

Amma: (embracing the child tightly and speaking in English) Amma call daddy.

At that point the father came close to Amma. He said that he had accidentally sat on the boy's hand that morning. This happened at home, and the little boy was trying to explain that to Amma.

Still holding the boy close to Her, Amma said, "Look, my baby, Amma is going to give a good whacking to your daddy, okay?"

The boy nodded his head. Amma acted as if She was beating the father, and the boy's father pretended to cry. Suddenly, the boy caught hold of Amma's hand and said, "Enough."

Holding the child more tightly, Amma laughed. The devotees joined in too.

Amma: Look, he loves his father. He doesn't want anyone to hurt his daddy.

Like this little boy, who came and opened his heart to Amma without any reservations, children, you too should learn how to pour out your hearts to God. Though Amma was only pretending to beat his father, for the boy it was real. He didn't want his father to feel hurt. Likewise, children, understand the pain of others and be compassionate to everyone.

Waking Up the Dreaming Disciple

Questioner: How does the Guru help the disciple transcend the ego?

Amma: By creating the necessary situations. In fact, it is the *Satguru's* [True Master's] compassion that helps the disciple.

Questioner: So, what exactly helps the disciple? The situations or the Guru's compassion?

Amma: The situations emerge as a result of the Satguru's infinite compassion.

Questioner: Are these situations normal situations or are they special?

Amma: They will be normal situations. However, they are also special because they are another form of the Satguru's blessing for the spiritual uplift of the disciple.

Questioner: Is there a conflict between the Guru and disciple during the process of removing the ego?

Amma: The mind will struggle and protest, because it wants to remain asleep and to continue dreaming. It doesn't want to be disturbed. However, a True Master is the disturber of the disciple's sleep. The Satguru's one and only aim is to awaken the disciple. So, there is a seeming contradiction. However, a true disciple endowed with *shraddha* [loving faith] will use discrimination to overcome such inner conflicts.

Obedience to the Guru

Questioner: Will perfect obedience to the Guru ultimately lead to the death of the ego?

Amma: Yes, it will. In the *Kathopanishad*, the *Satguru* [True Master] is represented by Yama, the Lord of Death. This is because the Guru symbolizes the death of the disciple's ego, which can take place only with the help of a Satguru.

Obedience to the Satguru comes from the disciple's love for the Guru. The disciple will feel tremendously inspired by the Master's self-sacrifice and compassion. Moved by this nature of the Guru, the disciple will remain spontaneously open and obedient in front of the Guru.

Questioner: It takes extraordinary courage to face the death of the ego, doesn't it?

Amma: Certainly, that is why very few are able to do it. Allowing the ego to die is like knocking at the door of death. That is what Nachiketas, the young seeker of the *Kathopanishad*, did. But if you have the courage and determination to knock at the door of death, you will find that there is no death. For even death, or the death of the ego, is an illusion.

The Horizon Is Here

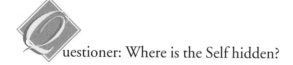

Questioner: Where is the Self hidden?

Amma: The question is like asking, "Where am I hidden?" You are not hidden anywhere. You are within you. Similarly, the Self is also within you and without.

From the seashore, it looks like the ocean and the horizon are meeting each other at one point. Suppose there is an island there, it appears that the trees are touching the sky. However, if we go there, do we see the meeting point? No, on the contrary, that point also moves away. Now it will be at another place. In reality where is the horizon? The horizon is right here where we stand, isn't it? Likewise, that which you are searching for is right here. But as long as we are hypnotized by our body and mind, it will remain far away.

As far as the supreme knowledge is concerned, you are like a beggar. The True Master appears and tells you, "Look, you own the entire universe. Throw away your begging bowl and look for the treasure hidden within you."

Your ignorance about reality makes you adamantly say, "You are talking nonsense. I am a beggar, and I want to continue begging for the rest of my life. Please leave me alone." However, a *Satguru* [True Master] won't leave you like that. The Satguru will keep reminding you of the same thing again and again until you are convinced and begin the search.

In short, the Satguru helps us to realize the begging state of the mind, urges us to throw away the begging bowl and assists us in becoming the owner of the universe.

Faith & Rosary

uring one Devi Bhava in San Ramon, California, I was about to go to sing *bhajans* [devotional songs], when a lady approached me with tears in her eyes.

She said, "I lost something that is very precious to me."

The lady sounded very desperate. She said, "I was sleeping upstairs on the balcony with the rosary that my grandma had given me. When I woke up, it was gone. Someone has stolen it. It was priceless to me. Oh, my God, what am I supposed to do now?" She began to cry.

"Did you search in the Lost and Found?" I inquired.

"Yes," she said, "but it wasn't there."

I said, "Please don't cry. Let's make an announcement. If somebody has found it or taken it by mistake, they may bring it back if you explain how precious it is to you."

I was about to lead her to the sound-system when she said, "How could this happen on a Devi Bhava night, when I came to have Amma's *darshan*?"

When I heard her say this, I spontaneously spoke the following words to her: "Look, you were not attentive enough. That is why you lost the rosary. Why did you sleep with the rosary in your hand if it was so precious to you? There are different types of people gathered here tonight. Amma discards none. She allows everyone to participate and be joyful. Knowing this, you should have taken better care of your rosary. Instead you are blaming Amma without shouldering the responsibility of being careless."

The lady was unconvinced. She said, "My faith in Amma is shaken."

I asked her, "Did you have any faith to lose? If you had any real faith, how could you lose it?"

She did not say anything. However, I directed her to the sound system and she made the announcement.

A couple of hours later when I finished singing, I met the lady at the main entrance to the hall. She was waiting to see me. The lady told me that she had found the rosary. In fact, somebody saw it lying on the balcony and took it, thinking that it was a gift for him from Amma. However, when he heard the announcement, he brought it back.

The lady said, "Thanks for your suggestion."

"Thank Amma, because She was so compassionate that She didn't want you to lose faith," I replied. Before I said goodbye to her, I told her, "Though there are different types of people here, they all love Amma; otherwise, you wouldn't have seen your rosary again."

Love & Surrender

Questioner: Amma, what is the difference between love and surrender?

Amma: Love is conditional. Surrender is unconditional.

Questioner: What does this mean?

Amma: In love, there is the lover and the beloved, disciple and Master, devotee and God. But in surrender, the two disappear. The Master alone is; God alone is.

Awareness & Alertness

Questioner: Is awareness the same as *shraddha* [love and faith]?

Amma: Yes, the more shraddha you have, the more aware you will be. Lack of awareness creates obstacles on the path to eternal freedom. It is like driving through the fog. You won't be able to see anything clearly. It is dangerous too, as an accident can occur at any time. On the other hand, actions that are done with awareness help you to realize your innate divinity. They help increase your clarity moment by moment.

Faith Makes Everything Simple

Questioner: Why is Self-realization so difficult to attain?

Amma: In fact, Self-realization is easy, because the Atman [Self] is the closest to us. It is the mind that makes it difficult.

Questioner: But that is not how it is described in the scriptures and by Great Masters. The means and methods are so rigorous.

Amma: The scriptures and the Great Masters always try to make it simple. They keep reminding you that the Self, or God, is your true nature, which means it is not far away. It is the real you, your original face. But you need to have faith to imbibe this truth. Faithlessness makes the path rigorous, and faith makes it simple. Tell a child, "You are a king," and within a second the child will identify with that and start acting like a king. Do grownups have such faith? No, they don't. Therefore it is difficult for them.

Focusing on the Goal

Questioner: Amma, how can one enhance one's spiritual journey?

Amma: Through sincere *sadhana* [spiritual practices] and focusing on the Goal. Always remember that your physical existence in this world is meant for spiritual attainment. Your thinking and living should be shaped in such a way that they help you progress on the path.

Questioner: Is focusing on the Goal the same as having detachment?

Amma: For one who is focused on the Goal, detachment automatically arises. For example, if you are traveling to another city where you have urgent business, your mind will be constantly fixed on your destination, won't it? You may see a beautiful park and a lake, a nice restaurant, a juggler who juggles with 15 balls and so forth, but will you be attracted to any of these? No. Your mind will be detached from these sights, and it will be attached to the destination. Likewise, if one has genuine focus on the Goal, detachment automatically follows.

Action and Bondage

Questioner: Some people believe that action creates obstructions on the spiritual path and, therefore, it is advisable to refrain from it. Is this correct?

Amma: That is probably a lazy man's definition. Karma [action], in itself, is not dangerous. However, when it is not combined with compassion, when it is used for self-gratification and only to fulfill ulterior motives, it becomes dangerous. For example, during surgery, a doctor should be fully aware and have a compassionate attitude too. Instead, if the doctor broods on troubles at home, his or her level of awareness goes down. This may even risk the patient's life. Such karma is *adharma* [incorrect action]. On the other hand, the sense of contentment the doctor derives from a successful surgery can help him or her rise higher, if it is directed properly. In other words, when karma is performed with awareness and compassion as its driving force, it accelerates one's spiritual journey. On the contrary, when we do things with little or no awareness and a lack of compassion, it becomes dangerous.

For Discrimination to Grow

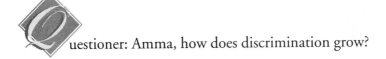

Questioner: Amma, how does discrimination grow?

Amma: Through contemplative action.

Questioner: Is a discriminative mind a matured mind?

Amma: Yes, a spiritually matured mind.

Questioner: Will such a mind have greater capacities?

Amma: Greater capacities and understanding.

Questioner: Understanding of what?

Amma: Understanding of everything, every situation and experience.

Questioner: You mean, even the negative and painful situations?

Answer: Yes, all. Even painful experiences when understood deeply have a positive effect on our life. Just beneath the surface of all experiences, whether good or bad, is the spiritual message. So viewing everything from outside is materialism and viewing everything from inside is spirituality.

The Final Leap

Questioner: Amma, is there a point in a seeker's life when he or she needs to simply wait?

Amma: Yes. After performing spiritual practices for a long time, which is after putting forth all necessary effort, there will come a point when the *sadhak* [spiritual seeker] has to stop all *sadhana* [spiritual practices] and wait patiently for the realization to happen.

Questioner: Can the seeker take the leap by him- or herself at that point?

Amma: No. In fact, that is a crucial point, when the sadhak needs immense help.

Questioner: Will the Guru provide that help?

Amma: Yes, only the *Satguru*'s [True Master's] grace can help the sadhak at that point. That is when the sadhak requires absolute patience. Because the sadhak has done whatever he or she could; all self-effort has been put forth. Now, the sadhak is helpless. He or she doesn't know how to take the last step. The seeker may even get confused at this point and turn back to the world, thinking that there is no such state as Self-realization. Only the Satguru's presence and grace will inspire the seeker and help him or her to transcend that state.

The Happiest Moment in Amma's Life

Questioner: Amma, what is the happiest moment in Your life?

Amma: Every moment.

Questioner: That means?

Amma: Amma means Amma is constantly happy, because there is only pure love as far as Amma is concerned.

Amma didn't speak for some time. The darshan went on. Then one devotee brought a picture of Goddess Kali dancing on Lord

Shiva's chest for Amma to bless. Amma showed the picture to the devotee in the question line.

Amma: Look at this picture. Though Kali looks fierce, she is in a blissful mood. Do you know why? Because she has just severed the head, the ego, of her beloved disciple. The head is considered to be the seat of the ego. Kali is celebrating that precious moment when her disciple has completely transcended his ego. One more soul who has long been wandering in darkness has been released from the clutches of *maya* [illusion].

When a person attains salvation, the *kundalini shakti* [spiritual energy] of the entire creation rises up and awakens. From then on he or she sees everything as divine. Thus the beginning of an endless celebration is triggered. So, Kali is dancing in ecstasy.

Questioner: Do You mean that for You too, the happiest moment is when Your children are able to go beyond their ego?

A beaming smile lit up Amma's face.

The Biggest Gift Amma Gives

One elderly devotee who had advanced cancer came for Amma's *darshan*. Knowing that he was going to die very soon, the man said, "Goodbye, Amma. Thank You so much for all that You have given me. You showered pure love on this child and showed me the way during this painful period. Without You, I would have collapsed long back. Always hold this soul close to You." Saying so, the devotee took Amma's hand and placed it on his chest.

The man then sobbed, covering his face in his cupped hands. Amma affectionately put him on Her shoulder, as She wiped the tears that trickled down Her own cheeks.

Lifting his head from Her shoulder, Amma looked deep into his eyes. He stopped crying. He looked even cheerful and strong. He said, "With all the love You have given me, Amma, Your child is not sad. My one and only concern is whether or not I will remain in Your lap even after death. That is why I cried. Otherwise, I am okay."

Gazing into his eyes with profound love and concern, Amma softly said, "Don't worry, my child. Amma assures that you will eternally remain in Her lap."

The man's face suddenly lit up with immense joy. He looked so peaceful. With eyes still wet, Amma silently watched him as he walked away.

Love Makes Everything Alive

uestioner: Amma, if everything is pervaded by consciousness, do non-living objects also have consciousness?

Amma: They have a consciousness, which you can't feel or understand.

Questioner: How can we understand that?

Amma: Through pure love. Love makes everything alive and conscious.

Questioner: I have love, but I don't see everything as alive and conscious.

Amma: That means there is something wrong with your love.

Questioner: Love is love. How can there be something wrong with love?

Amma: True love is that which helps us experience life and the life-force everywhere. If your love doesn't enable you to see this, such love is not real love. It is illusory love.

Questioner: But this is something that is so difficult to understand and practice, isn't it so?

Amma: No, it is not.

The devotee remained quiet with a puzzled look on her face.

Amma: It is not as difficult as you think. In fact, almost everyone does it. However, they are not aware of it.

Just then, one of the devotees brought her cat to be blessed by Amma. Amma stopped speaking for a while. She affectionately held the cat for a few moments and caressed it. She then carefully applied some sandal paste to its forehead and fed it one Hershey's Kiss.

Amma: Boy or girl?

Questioner: Girl.

Amma: What is her name?

Questioner: Rose…. (with great concern) She has not been feeling well for the last two days. Please bless her, Amma, for a speedy recovery. She is my faithful friend and companion.

As the lady uttered these words, tears welled up in her eyes. Amma lovingly rubbed some sacred ash on the cat and handed it back to the devotee, who left Amma's presence happy.

Amma: For that daughter, her cat is not one among millions of cats; her cat is unique. It is almost like a human being to her. As far as she is concerned, her "Rose" has an individuality of its own. Why? Because she loves the cat so much. She is tremendously identified with it.

People all over the world do this, don't they? They name their cats, dogs, parrots and sometimes even trees. Once they name it and make it their own, for that particular person, the animal, bird or plant becomes distinctive and different from others of its species. Suddenly it assumes the status of something more than a mere creature. That individual's identification with it gives it a new life.

Look at small children. A doll becomes a living and concious thing for them. They converse with the doll, feed it and sleep with it. What gives life to the doll? The child's love for it, isn't it? Love can transform even a mere object into a living and conscious thing.

Now tell, Amma, is such love difficult?

A Great Lesson in Forgiveness

Questioner: Amma, is there anything that You want to tell me now? Any special instructions for me at this point in my life?

Amma: (smiling) Be patient.

Questioner: Is that all?

Amma: That is a lot.

The devotee had turned around and taken a few steps away when Amma called out to him, "...and have forgiveness too."

Hearing Amma's words, the man turned around and asked, "Are You talking to me?"

Amma: Yes, to you.

The man came back near Amma's seat.

Questioner: I am sure You are giving me some hint, as that has always been my experience in the past. Amma, please tell me clearly what You are suggesting.

Amma continued giving darshan while the man waited to hear more. For some time She didn't say anything.

Amma: There must be something, some incident or situation that suddenly surfaced in your mind. Otherwise, why did you react so quickly when you heard Amma saying "forgiveness"? Son, you didn't have the same reaction when Amma told you "be patient." You accepted it and had started to walk away, didn't you? So something is really bothering you.

Hearing Amma's words, the man sat quietly for some time with his head hung low. Suddenly, he began to weep, covering his face with his hands. Amma couldn't bear the sight of Her child crying. She affectionately wiped his tears and rubbed his chest.

Amma: Don't worry, son. Amma is with you.

Questioner: (sobbing) You are right. I am unable to forgive my son. I have not spoken to him for the past year. I am deeply hurt and very angry at him. Amma, please help.

Amma: (glancing compassionately at the devotee) Amma understands.

Questioner: About a year ago he came home one day hopelessly stoned. When I questioned his behavior, he became violent and shouted at me, and then he started smashing plates and destroying things. I completely lost my patience and threw him out of the house. Since then, I have neither seen nor spoken to him.

The man seemed really miserable.

Amma: Amma sees your heart. Anyone would have lost control in that situation. Don't carry any guilty feelings about the incident. However, it is important for you to forgive him.

Questioner: I want to, but I am incapable of forgetting and moving forward. Whenever my heart tells me to forgive him, my mind questions it. My mind says, "Why should you forgive him? He committed the mistake, so let him come to regret it and seek your forgiveness."

Amma: Son, do you really wish to resolve the situation?

Questioner: Yes, Amma. I want to, and I want to help heal my son and myself.

Amma: If so, never listen to your mind. The mind cannot heal or resolve any such situation. On the contrary, the mind will aggravate it and confuse you more.

Questioner: Amma, what is Your advice?

Amma: Amma may not be able to say what you want to hear. However, Amma can tell you what will really help you to heal the situation and bring peace between you and your son. Have trust and things will gradually straighten out.

Questioner: Kindly instruct me, Amma. I will try my best to do whatever You say.

Amma: Whatever has happened has happened. Allow yourself to believe and accept that first. Then, trust that beyond the known cause there was also an unknown cause for the chain of events that took place that day. Your mind is uncompromising and eager to blame your son for everything. Fine. Regarding that particular incident, maybe he was to blame. Nevertheless....

Questioner: (anxiously) Amma, You didn't finish what You were going to say.

Amma: Let Amma ask you a question. Have you been very respectful and loving to your parents, your father in particular?

Questioner: (looking somewhat puzzled) With my mother, yes, I had a very beautiful relationship... but with my father, I had a terrible relationship.

Amma: Why?

Questioner: Because he was very strict, and I found it difficult to accept his ways.

Amma: And of course there were times when you were very rude to him, which hurt his feelings, isn't it so?

Question: Yes.

Amma: That means what you have done to your father is now coming back to you in the form of your son, his words and deeds.

Questioner: Amma, I trust Your words.

Amma: Son, didn't you suffer quite a lot because of your strained relationship with your father?

Questioner: Yes, I did.

Amma: Did you ever forgive him and heal the relationship?

Questioner: Yes, but only a few days before his death.

Amma: Son, do you want your son to go through the same suffering, which in turn will bring misery to you as well?

The man burst into tears as he shook his head and said, "No, Amma, no… never."

Amma: (holding him close) So, forgive your son, because that is the way to peace and love.

The man sat beside Amma and meditated for a long time. When he left, he said, "I feel so light and relaxed. I am going to meet my son as soon as possible. Thank You, Amma. Thank You so much."

Darshan

Questioner: How should people approach You in order to get Your *darshan* strongly?

Amma: How do we strongly experience the beauty and fragrance of a flower? By remaining completely open to the flower. Suppose you have a stuffy nose? You will miss it. In a similar manner, if your mind is blocked with judging thoughts and preconceived ideas, you will miss Amma's darshan.

A scientist looks at a flower as an object for experimentation; a poet, as inspiration for a poem. What about a musician? He sings about the flower. And an herbalist will see it as the source of an effective medicine, isn't it so? For an animal or an insect, it is nothing but food. None of them see the flower as a flower, as a whole. Likewise, people are of different natures. Amma receives everyone equally—gives them all the same opportunity, the same love, the same darshan. She discards none, because all are Her children. However, depending on the receptivity of the receiver, darshan will be different.

Darshan is always there. It is a never-ending flow. You just have to receive it. If you can completely withdraw from your mind for at least one second, darshan in all its fullness will happen.

Questioner: In that sense, does everyone receive Your darshan?

Amma: It depends how open the person is. The more open, the more darshan they receive. Though not fully, everyone receives a glimpse.

Questioner: A glimpse of what?

Amma: A glimpse of what they really are.

Questioner: Does it mean they will get a glimpse of what You really are as well?

Amma: The reality in both you and in Amma is the same.

Questioner: What is that?

Amma: The blissful silence of love.

Not Thinking, But Trusting

Reporter: Amma, what is Your purpose for being here on this planet?

Amma: What is *your* purpose for being here on this planet?

Reporter: I have set goals in my life. I think I am here to accomplish them.

Amma: Amma too is here to fulfill certain goals that are beneficial to society. However, unlike you, Amma not only *thinks* that those goals will be achieved, Amma has complete trust that those goals will be attained.